The School Reform Landscape

Fraud, Myth, and Lies

Christopher H. Tienken
and
Donald C. Orlich

Published in Partnership with the
American Association of School Administrators

ROWMAN & LITTLEFIELD EDUCATION
A division of
ROWMAN & LITTLEFIELD PUBLISHERS, INC.
Lanham • New York • Toronto • Plymouth, UK

Published in partnership with the American Association of School Administrators

Published by Rowman & Littlefield Education
A division of Rowman & Littlefield Publishers, Inc.
A wholly owned subsidiary of The Rowman & Littlefield Publishing Group, Inc.
4501 Forbes Boulevard, Suite 200, Lanham, Maryland 20706
www.rowman.com

10 Thornbury Road, Plymouth PL6 7PP, United Kingdom

British Library Cataloguing in Publication Information Available

Library of Congress Cataloging-in-Publication Data

Tienken, Christopher.
The school reform landscape : fraud, myth, and lies / Christopher H. Tienken and Donald C. Orlich.
pages cm
Published in partnership with the American Association of School Administrators.
Includes bibliographical references and index.
ISBN 978-1-4758-0257-3 (cloth : alk. paper) — ISBN 978-1-4758-0258-0 (pbk. : alk. paper) — ISBN 978-1-4758-0259-7 (electronic)
1. Public schools—United States. 2. School improvement programs—United States. 3. Education and state—United States. I. Orlich, Donald C. II. American Association of School Administrators. III. Title.
LA212.T54 2013
371.010973—dc23
2012046746

♾™ The paper used in this publication meets the minimum requirements of American National Standard for Information Sciences Permanence of Paper for Printed Library Materials, ANSI/NISO Z39.48-1992.

Printed in the United States of America

Contents

Foreword

C. M. Achilles, EdD

According to Gustav Schwab (1946), much of the early accounts of the progress of humankind can be attributed to the study of the myths and epics of Western civilization, especially of the Greeks. Two major players in the early events were Prometheus (foresight) and his less well-known brother, Epimetheus (afterthought). One key point this story brings to us is that the future builds upon the past, or at least in the future those who advocate for progress should acknowledge its heritage.

One way to accomplish this feat in the education policy arena is for writers to join forces to present their views on past and current social forces exerting much pressure on education in the United States. The coauthors of this volume published by Rowman & Littlefield Education have combined their talents to provide a highly accessible critical review of some threshold education reform issues. The authors provide a look at some of the current and past myths that populate the reform landscape. Because education is cumulative throughout our lives, it should be framed as essentially a lifetime of discovery. As such, this volume assists current and future education leaders to discover the foresight and afterthought necessary to discern the truth from myth and the facts from lies that continue to drive education policy and practice.

The humorist/philosopher H. L. Mencken is reputed to have said, "For every complex question there is a simple answer—and it is wrong" (See Carson et al., 1991). In a similar vein, the philosopher George Santayana, citing the Roman philosopher Cicero, explained that those who cannot remember the past are condemned to repeat it. Consider Plato's myth of the cave! Things are not always what they seem at first: each point, pro and con, needs to be explored using the lenses of empirical facts, theoretical frameworks, and philosophical foundations. Such is the current landscape of education reform policies and practices.

Mencken's and Santayana's expressions taken together suggest that humans should study and know the past so they can improve the future. That is a large part of the purpose for education—to leave the world a better place by examining *What Is* and encouraging people to influence *What May Be* positive changes, while maintaining and advocating what research and practices have shown to contribute to social harmony and growth. One way to activate this challenge is for competent researchers to analyze education policies carefully and publish their conclusions for others to review or analyze deeply. Education must satisfactorily meet the norms of the diverse cultures within which it operates. Is the quality of U.S. public education policy better, worse, or the same as in 2008, 2000, or 1992 for that matter?

Amid much disturbing national and world news these days, I'm pleased to see a collaborative effort by two scholars who review some major reports and policies in education and society in general and suggest alternative views about the continuing assault on American public education by big business, government, and advocacy groups. Christopher Tienken from Seton Hall University (SHU) in New Jersey and Donald Orlich, a professor emeritus from Washington State University (WSU), combined their talents to continue the important work of Gerald Bracey, PhD, and others who worked diligently to present a balanced picture of education in America, and explain the need for a carefully educated citizenry in a democracy, or to paraphrase Thomas Jefferson, "If a nation wishes to be ignorant and free, it wishes what never has been and never will be."

Professors Tienken and Orlich have traced some major education and cultural factors that educators should consider as they progress both in advancing knowledge and confronting social values such as freedom of choice and charter schools. For example, how do charter schools resonate with the *Brown v. Board of Education* Supreme Court decision? Is a legalized return to segregated schools disguised as charter schools imminent? For those interested in curriculum and assessment, the authors critique the Common Core State Standards and national testing to find that the emperor might not have clothes.

Although charter schools, standardized curriculum, and standardized testing have been generally accepted in some form by most professional organizations and educators, the profession as a whole seems woefully uninformed regarding the empirical facts on such subjects. Jack Culbertson, PhD, longtime director of the University Council for Education Administration, has warned educators to evaluate thoroughly what they advocate and do: perhaps to make haste slowly (*festina lente*).

> However, the last century has taught us pertinent lessons, two of which are noted. Borrowed concepts tend to enter textbooks before they are adequately tested in school systems. The result is that such concepts may be used indefinitely in training programs even though their actual relations to school management and leadership practices remain unknown. (p. 107)

The Culbertson (1990) warning seems to have classical roots in the myth of Prometheus, the forward-looking brother, and his lesser-known brother, Epimetheus (afterthought or hindsight). Don't take the analogies too lightly. I believe that this book will satisfy a need in the education literature of today by challenging the status quo with evidence. The publishers, Rowman & Littlefield Education, have found a niche and a writing team who will fill the void with challenging perspectives.

REFERENCES

Carson, C. C., Hueleskamp, R. M. & Woodall, T. D. (May 10, 1991). *Perspectives on Education in America. Annotated Briefing, Third Draft.* Sandia National Laboratories, Albuquerque, NM. Esp. A Call to Action, pp. 2–9. *Note:* Education was such a hot topic at the time of this report from an esteemed federal laboratory that the Reagan administration tried to downplay this report's generally positive outlook about U.S. education, and the lab was told to recall the document. (You bury this report, or we'll bury you. Quite a threat to a government-funded entity.)

Culbertson, J. A. (1990). Tomorrow's Challenges to Today's Professors of Educational Administration. *Record in Educational Administration and Supervision.* Fall/Winter. pp. 100–107.

Schwab, G. (1946). *Gods on Heroes: Myths and Epics of Ancient Greece.* New York: Pantheon Publishers. Esp. pp. 31–36 in re: Prometheus.

Preface

We wrote this book partially as a rebuttal to education bureaucrats, neoliberal policy wonks, some legislators, and other misguided parties who propose, support, and administer education policies and practices born from fear, mythology, and lies. Simply put, we grew weary of hearing yet another person calling for a "Sputnik" moment in education without understanding that Sputnik was actually proof of American technological superiority. As we imply with the title, we present a critical and some might say contrarian analysis of some school reform initiatives proposed since the Russians' launch of that little steel ball in 1957. We scrutinize school reform events, proposals, and policies from the last 60 years through the lens of critical social theory and experimentalist philosophy and examine the tensions between the need to keep a vibrant democratic and unitary system of public education and the ongoing assault by corporate and elite interests in creating a dual system of privilege and potential repression.

We organized the book into nine chapters. Chapter 1 presents an overview of the historic purposes of public education and the seemingly never-ending struggle between reformers who believed public education should indeed serve the public good, and those who believed that the wealthy should receive a more comprehensive education while the masses remain subjected to a mechanistic structure of cultural reproduction and knowledge imitation.

In chapters 2 through 8 we critique the following events, proposals, and policies: (a) Sputnik, (b) *A Nation At Risk*, (c) big business values in education, (d) No Child Left Behind, (e) state standards movement, (f) Common Core State Standards initiative, (g) high-stakes testing, and (h) charter schools. We provide an evidence-based examination of some free-market education reform ideas and pierce the veil of newer policies to find that they are built not upon empirical evidence, but instead rest solidly on a foundation of ideology.

In the final part of the book, chapter 9, we present ideas for a new set of reform policies, based on empirical evidence and supportive of a unitary system of education aimed at nurturing students into a participative democracy by educating them democratically. It is our hope that readers will maintain an open mind as they reflect upon our messages in this book.

Acknowledgments

This book explores some of what we call the myths, frauds, and lies of the school reform landscape since Sputnik I. Our ideas and insights on school reform were sharpened by our families and friends. We would like to thank those in our professional lives who have the courage to use science, empathy, and love to serve the best interests of children and give a voice to the voiceless. To those in our personal lives, words are a poor substitute for our gratitude, but we offer them so others can catch a small glimpse of what you mean to us. We wish to acknowledge the many colleagues who provided us the tools to complete this manuscript. We especially wish to thank the authors, editors and researchers who gave us inspiration and the permission to cite their works in detail. We acknowledge gratefully the support from our Rowman & Littlefield Education editors, Carlie Wall and Dr. Thomas Koerner. Their patience is truly a virtue.

CHRISTOPHER H. TIENKEN

I have been fortunate in my career to work with school administrators and teachers who stand out in their commitment to children. They take stances for children that some call contrarian when they oppose repressive policies that seek to bifurcate the unitary system into special schools for the wealthy and lesser institutions for the not so wealthy. They are what Charles Achilles calls the defenders of the defenseless. I benefit greatly from my ongoing relationships with leaders like Ralph Ferrie, Patrick Michel, Thomas Tramaglini, Patricia Gasparini, Keynon Kummings, Jennifer Luff, and others.

As a professor I have been lucky enough to have ongoing interactions with Yong Zhao from the University of Oregon. Yong's refreshing and innovative approach to leadership and education policy continues to bend my mind and cause me to reflect. His work breathes life into the reductionist policy environment and provides evidence of the power of creation over imitation. I would be remiss if I did not thank the Seton Hall University Department of Education Leadership, Management, and Policy for their ongoing support and guidance. Their high expectations and coaching provides the environment needed to take risks and grow. Thanks to Tharinee Kamnoetsin for her careful reviews of this book. Fortunately, I had Daniel Tanner to guide my initial foray into curriculum and instruction research. His advice has been invaluable to my professional growth. I am grateful to call Charles M. Achilles my mentor. Chuck continues to shape my work and my thinking. His work on the Tennessee STAR Study in particular changed the face of education research and improved the lives of untold numbers of children. He is an inspiration and a role model.

In my personal life I am lucky enough to have parents and a sister who take an interest in my work. Thanks to Pappy for keeping me grounded and for his appreciation of snow. God bless Lucille. There are also those special places that inspire ideas, refresh the spirit, and bring clarity: Sanctuary I and II, San Giovanni Montebello, the Campo, and Lido Sole.

Although you won't see them listed as authors, my wife Allison and daughters Gabriella and Francesca influenced large portions of this book. The joy of experiencing life through the eyes of a child is eclipsed only by the unconditional love of a wife. Love makes all things possible.

DONALD C. ORLICH

The following individuals encouraged me to continue my thoughts on the issues of school reform. Mr. Jack Horne has provided ideas and Dr. Gene Sharatt has been very supportive of my work to show the real issues addressing school reform.

Several colleagues and friends at the University of Montana's Phyllis J. Washington College of Education and Human Sciences provided information and encouragement to complete the work. And, my understanding wife, Patricia, has been a strong supporter. Finally, thanks to all the educators and citizens who fight to keep our public schools open to all.

Introduction

To understand where public education policy and practices fit into the current iteration of school reform it is important to know where public education has been and how things arrived at this place. In the first part of the book, we begin the process of unpacking modern school reform by providing an overview of the historical purposes and roles of public education in the United States. Our purpose is not to create an exhaustive review of education reform or the history of public education in the United States; Tanner and Tanner (2007) already accomplished that task. Our intent is to give readers the background knowledge necessary to engage in an analysis of the current reform landscape in terms of its recent historical roots so they can better evaluate present and future school reform proposals and understand our ideas for change.

We use the terms school *reform* and *reformers* in two ways throughout this book. One way we use the terms is to describe processes and people that attempt to deride and degrade, without empirical evidence, the quality of public education in the United States. We provide evidence throughout the book of how the detractors of the unitary U.S. public school system use misinformation, ideology, rhetoric, and/or less than accurate statistics to forward a thinly veiled agenda of creating a dual system of education. Some are actively building a system that favors those who "have" over those who "have not."

The creation of a two-tiered, dual system, if not stopped, will eventually leave the traditional unitary public school system with less public funding and support and a greater concentration of economically disadvantaged students and students with special needs. It is already happening in the nation's urban areas. The siphoning of less poor and less cognitive and linguistically needy students has already begun to create a system of "haves" and "have-nots" under the umbrella of "public school."

The other way we use the terms *reform* and *reformer* is to highlight positive efforts to improve schooling. The commingling of the "good" with the "bad" is purposeful because school "reformers" approach public education policy formation from at least two different camps. There are those who propose and have proposed changes to the system that we find undemocratic and harmful to the long-term health of education and democracy, whereas there are others whose proposals were or would be helpful to create a more participative and democratic country for children and adults.

Our premise is that people concerned with safeguarding the democratic and unifying institution of public education must dig below the rhetoric and surface arguments of reform proposals and decipher if the proposed reforms and the reformers advocate changes to benefit the greater good or if the changes are something less than good for the population. We do some of that work in this book. The rest is up to the reader.

LENSES OF REFORM

The unpacking process requires that we choose a framework from which to view and critique school reform initiatives, policies, and practices. The choice of a framework is inherently biased based on those who do the choosing. Our biases include a respect and preference for a participatory democracy led by people who develop policies, institutions, and cultural norms that promote the attainment of "liberty and justice for all" in an equitable society. We hold a bias against state- and corporate-sponsored education reform initiatives or policies that overtly or covertly structure public education in ways that favor one group over others or that have the potential to create long-term structural inequities in our societal systems. We believe public education reformers should not impede access to the opportunities needed to achieve "liberty and justice for all" as a nation of diverse peoples. Our biases lead us to examine school reform through the lens of critical social theory (Freire, 2000) and the experimentalist philosophy.

Specifically, we use critical social theory as a way to critique and examine school reform and its influences on the ability of children, especially those who are members of groups not in the racial majority or wealthy minority, to overcome state-sponsored policies, institutions, and norms that lead to intended or unintended consequences that foster inequality of opportunity. In its most basic terms, critical social theory requires one to examine the formal structures that exist in society and to be skeptical of those structures unless evidence demonstrates that the structures facilitate upward mobility and equity.

Freire (2000) coined the phrase "Banking Model" to describe education policies and practices that seek to deposit static information from the ruling class into the heads of children from the nonruling classes as a way to keep the current social structure, whatever that might be, in place for the foreseeable future. Standardized, mandated socially inert curriculum, enforced with standardized, mandated testing, is one way that policy makers apply the Banking Model. People with resources (money) usually do not subject their children to this type of model, as they can afford other "options" or have the state pay for those options through voucher programs or other types of schools that take public money but do not serve all students.

We use critical social theory as a lens to examine policies and practices to determine whether those policies and practices can facilitate the attainment of "liberty and justice for all" or if they lead to balkanizing and siloing, along economic and racial lines. We will apply this critical skepticism to the modern school reform movement, and demonstrate with qualitative and quantitative evidence that things are not what they always seem on the surface in terms of recent reform initiatives and that those who share our biases should be concerned and seek to take action.

We caution our readers not to mistake our approach as one-sided. It is not. Our approach, through the use of social critical theory, requires we look through an evidence-based lens. For example, the empirical evidence, evidence derived via recognized scientific methods, suggests that current criticisms of the public school system as a "failing" institution that needs to be replaced with a system of choice and options are flawed. The evidence suggests there has been a manufactured crisis (Berliner & Biddle, 1995). We will examine critically some of the more common criticisms of public education that, although false, seem to permeate society as fact and lead to the development of policies and practices that jeopardize the unitary system.

In chapter 1, we present a general overview of public education and attempt to explain the basic tension between the unitary- and dual-system proponents. It is a tension that has existed since the genesis of public schooling in America and continues today.

REFERENCES

Berliner, D. C. & Biddle, B. J. (1995). *The Manufactured Crisis: Myths, Frauds and the Attack on America's Public Schools.* Reading, MA: Addison-Wesley.

Freire, P. (2000). *Pedagogy of the Oppressed: 30th Anniversary Edition.* New York: Continuum.

Tanner, D. & Tanner, L. (2007). *Curriculum Development: Theory into Practice.* New York: Allyn & Bacon.

ONE

Liberty and Justice for All

Since the formation of the United States of America, there has been debate over the roles and purposes of education. Some envisioned a public education system that unified diverse people on a level playing field, in the spirit of all men being created equal. Others sought a dual system of education based on the European model in which children from the privileged ruling class received a more exclusive education, usually private, or a more comprehensive public version.

Children from the lower classes were remanded to a more mechanized, impersonal system of education based on a narrow curriculum, memorization, rote drill, and oral recitation. Some students of education history might list the Lancaster Model as one such example, although there are many others.

Proponents of a democratic, free system of schools viewed public education as the great equalizer, the way to bring about maximum vertical mobility within the social classes while developing a participative democracy with the representative republic model. It was a way to break out of the European class system and create an educated citizenry. Conversely, proponents of the dual system believed that the cultivation of a ruling class was important to the future of a strong central government and nation.

These early ideas of education reflected closely the political views of the Federalists and Anti-Federalists. The theme of conflict between the vision of a unitary system of public schools for everyone versus a dual system of private schools, semiprivate schools, and special academies for the privileged and a stripped-down public system for the "rest" has been a reoccurring one and continues today in America.

The conflict is played out in the "school reform" arguments with proponents lining up on either side of ideas like charter schools, school choice, vouchers, national curricula, standardized testing, specialized schools, and virtual schools. Proponents of the unitary system fight for equality and equity whereas proponents of the dual system fight to preserve privilege and elitism. This is a fight that continues today and serves as an unending backdrop to education reform both past and present.

UNIFYING VIEWS OF EDUCATION

The Jeffersonian view of the role and responsibility of education was one of equity, progress, change, and evolution. Jefferson's well-known flaws in his thinking on racial equality notwithstanding, he did propose and work to establish a public education system that would level the playing field between those that came from a more privileged background and those who did not have such advantages, so as to help society progress. Jefferson's first formal call for a public education system came in 1776 when he attempted to push a bill through the Virginia legislature that would have established a free public education system (Jewett, 1997).

Although the Virginia legislature did not pass the bill at that time, Jefferson did not waver on his support and belief in the creation of a system of common schools, and he worked to get the foundation for a public school system in the western territories included in the Ordinances of 1785 and 1787. The Ordinances guaranteed public support for education in any new states formed in the territory (Williams, 1989). By now most know of Jefferson's statement, "If a nation expects to be ignorant and free in a state of civilization, it expects what never was and never will be" (Padover, 1939). Jefferson's view of education was not lost after his presidency. James Carter continued the struggle for one system of public education in the New England states. Carter, a teacher and state legislator from Massachusetts, brought attention to the condition of public schools during the 1820s. Carter thought that if the public school was going to survive, its form and function needed to be reformed. Carter called for formal teacher training institutions, supported by the state, to professionalize public school teaching (Tanner & Tanner, 2007).

Like Jefferson before him, Carter advocated for free, public secondary schools and fought against the dual system of education that favored the rich and shunned children of lower social classes. At that time, there were secondary school academies for the wealthy, but nothing substantial existed in terms of a free public secondary school system. He railed against the teaching methods of the times that relied upon rote drill and memorization and called for new textbooks that would engage the students and bring science into the schools.

Carter's persistence paid off in 1839 when the first public normal schools opened in Massachusetts. Perhaps Carter's greatest contribution was his idea that the state should oversee and help direct the public school system to ensure a more equitable situation rather than relying solely on town control of education. He brought the idea of local control with state regulation to the policy discussion. This idea of state direction of a unitary system of public education laid a foundation for the later work of other proponents of the free public school system.

We can't discuss Carter's achievements without acknowledging the work of Horace Mann and Henry Barnard. Mann and Barnard worked to solidify a public school system in Massachusetts and Connecticut respectively. They built upon and extended Carter's proposals as they advocated for, and eventually founded, teacher education institutions to raise the quality of instruction taking place in classrooms. Mann advocated for the role of school principal as someone who could help improve the teaching that took place in classrooms and as someone who would be responsible for helping to develop a quality curriculum.

Mann understood the importance of heterogeneous grouping in public schools as a unifying practice to bring together students of diverse backgrounds. He was not naïve in his understandings of how a public school system could improve and support democracy. Mann knew that a public school system, in and of itself, could not sustain a democracy without careful thought about what that system would provide in the way of curriculum. In his view it was important that the system worked to develop people who could question, think critically, and strategize in order to grow the democratic republic. Mann stressed the importance of a curriculum that went beyond the basics of the time.

Mann realized that if the public school system was going to live up to its role as the equalizer of social classes and preparer of the next generation of democratic citizens, it needed a curriculum that fostered a well-rounded person prepared for the world that would be, not focused solely on the world as the way it is now. Thus, Mann fought for the inclusion of music, physical education, and the study of social issues (Mann, 1848), subjects that help to develop creative thinking and innovation. Keep in mind that the idea of an expanded curriculum was revolutionary at that time, as most public schools taught only writing, reading, arithmetic, and oral recitations.

Thanks in part to Jefferson, Carter, Barnard, Mann, and many others, a more "progressive" conception of education began to take shape during the first 80 years of the republic. However, as seems to be the case, for every hard-won battle to take several steps forward, there is always a step backward. That step back came in the form of Joseph Lancaster and monitorial instruction. The Lancasterian method, as alluded to earlier, originated in London, England, in a school opened for poor children and was quickly brought to large cities in the United States, New York being one of the first.

Proponents of the method placed large numbers of students in a class, 50 not being uncommon (Rayman, 1981). The teacher followed a scripted drill lesson and then turned the monitoring of instruction over to several "bright" students in the room. Each "bright" student was responsible to monitor a row of students. Then the teacher would move to another room, deliver instruction, and the process would continue. The method was cost efficient but highly mechanical and usually resulted in city children being subjected to it. Fortunately monitorial instruction faded from the scene, and by around 1850 it was no longer in vogue, but the idea of creating larger classes to maximize resources survives today.

Quincy

The battle against the dual system of education continued, but the free public school system continued to grow. The town of Quincy, Massachusetts, was the site of the next great contribution to the unitary system and the systemic development of liberty and justice for all through a free and quality public education system. Referred as the father of modern Progressivism by John Dewey, Francis Parker became the superintendent of Quincy schools in 1875.

At Quincy he found a school system with curriculum and instructional practices based on memorization and recitation. The students could not answer questions or read passages not previously rehearsed and were unable to engage in real problem solving, strategizing, or socially conscious critical thinking (Campbell, 1967). Parker initiated a series of curricular reforms that would transform public education in Quincy and beyond.

Parker instituted curriculum and instruction methods such as open-ended conversations, divergent questioning, the use of field trips to increase experiential learning, integrated language arts, and a correlated curriculum that fostered connections and transfer of knowledge and skills between subjects. He worked to create a curriculum and instruction program that introduced content in more meaningful ways that were connected to the students through problem posing. The Quincy system, as some referred to it (Campbell, 1967), demonstrated that quality can be a hallmark of public schools and that a dual system of schools was unnecessary.

Dewey Speaks

The undercurrents of democracy versus elitism and privilege as part of the school reform history continued throughout the 1800s. For every democratic gain there was pushback by undemocratic forces. John Dewey provided ongoing support for the important connection between a healthy public school system and a thriving representative democracy (Dewey, 1916). Dewey made many contributions to the developing public education system. We could not possibly do justice to all his accomplishments, nor will we try. Our purpose for bringing him into the discussion is to give the reader an insight into Dewey's ideas of democracy and the role of public education to support and nurture a democratic society.

Dewey's conception of the connection between democracy and schooling and Freire's Critical Social Theory (Freire, 2000), along with the champions of public schooling mentioned earlier, form the foundation for our thinking about public school and school reform.

Although Dewey authored a pantheon of education publications, we find poignant and important guidance for school reform in three of his works: *My Pedagogic Creed* (Dewey, 1897), *School and Society* (Dewey, 1899), and *Democracy and Education* (Dewey, 1916). Dewey (1897) stated, "I believe that education is the fundamental method of social progress and reform" (p. 80). In Dewey's mind, there could be no social progress, no national democratic progress, without quality democratic education for all children. But what was his conception of democracy and progress?

This is important to understand because even in a democracy, education can be used as an ultranationalist tool as we saw after Sputnik, during the Cold War, and now again with the "war on terrorism." It is one's conception of democracy that matters, because it is that conception that drives action. Dewey saw democracy as a social process, something related to the greater good, but also as something deeply personal, connected to informed and thoughtful action.

Democracy, as conceived by Dewey (1916), is "a way of personal life controlled not merely by faith in human nature but by faith in the capacity of human being for intelligent judgment and action if proper conditions are furnished" (p. 227). It was an idea that a public school system should develop the individual to the best of his or her potential so that individual could study the problems of democracy, of his or her community and nation, so as to take appropriate action to improve the greater good.

Dewey saw all members of the nation playing a part in the democracy, not just the privileged few making decisions for the "rest" of society. That is why it was important to Dewey, and others working for a unitary system, that there was a thriving public school system where the privileged and less privileged worked and learned side by side, just as they will have to do after they leave school.

Dewey reminds us that all members of the society need to be engaged in socially conscious, problem-based authentic learning and not just receive an inferior education based on recitation and mindless acceptance of a disjointed body of facts. If we wish to craft problem solvers, strategists, informed citizens, and a population that questions the status quo in order to improve it, then all students must be provided that type of education. Otherwise, we create a dual society of those given the mental tools and those who do the work for those who possess the tools. Dewey (1899) warned us:

> Plato somewhere speaks of the slave as one who in his actions does not express his own ideas, but those of some other man. It is our social problem now, even more urgent than in the time of Plato, that method, purpose, understanding, shall exist in the consciousness of the one who does the work, that his activity shall have meaning to himself. (pp. 37–38)

REPORTS, COMMISSIONS, AND LANDMARK STUDIES

Whereas some progressive educators viewed the roles and responsibilities of education as defender of democracy, social equalizer, and vehicle to realize liberty and justice for all through an expanded, thought-provoking curriculum connected to children and society, the messages coming out of the various formal committees and commissions were sometimes mixed.

For example, the *Report of the Committee of Ten on Secondary School Studies* (1893) recommended reforms to the high school curriculum that were on one hand aimed at strengthening the democracy, yet were autocratic in nature because they were geared more toward college entrance requirements at a time when less than 5 percent of the population graduated from high school. Driven by the concerns of the president of Harvard, Charles W. Eliot, the Committee of Ten was formed. Eliot was concerned that the elementary and secondary schools were taking too long to prepare students for college. Eliot wanted to compress the time it took students to work their way through the traditional elementary and secondary programs in an effort to bring down the average age of freshmen entering the university.

The curriculum proposed by the Committee of Ten was highly programmed and based in part on mental discipline, the belief that there was one set of high school courses that prepared students better for college than other options. Students were required to take four years of Latin and/or Greek, English literature and composition, math, and history. The report called for three years of science, the same science for everyone. There was little room for electives and even those were prescribed. Although the report was supposed to be aimed at reforming secondary education, it actually did more to promote the existing mechanistic system.

The proposed high school curriculum included none of the creative subjects like art, music, or physical education advocated by Mann. In fact, the opposite occurred, and the mechanistic view of high school curriculum became entrenched as a new set of high school graduation requirements. Stunningly, we hear similar proposals today as some vend and market the idea of one best path through high school.

Two years later in 1895, Eliot was back to reform the elementary school curriculum. Thus, the Committee of Fifteen was born. A major contribution of the Committee's work was the reduction of elementary schooling from ten to eight years, thus ultimately decreasing the entrance age of college freshmen, as desired by Eliot. Like the Committee of Ten before it, the report from the members of the Committee of Fifteen unknowingly cemented a mechanistic and segmented view of elementary school.

The recommendations from the members of the Committee of Fifteen prescribed, down to the minute, each subject at each grade level, along with the number of lessons per week for each subject. Once again, a reform aimed at improving education for all students actually had the unintended consequence of creating a straightjacketed elementary school experience.

The National Education Association's (NEA) Commission on the Reorganization of Secondary Education released the *Cardinal Principles of Secondary Education* in 1918. Recognizing that the previous reforms advocated by the members of the Committees of Ten and Fifteen were counterproductive to educating more children more effectively, the authors of the *Cardinal Principles* advocated a more democratic, socially conscious, problem-based approach based on the tenets of the progressive/experimentalist philosophy.

The *Cardinal Principles* came down squarely on the side of democracy, liberty, and justice for all through a unitary system of education that should attempt to connect content to students. The authors identified the crucial role of public education as the only public service capable of unifying the country around the ideals of democracy. It was the only public entity in which all citizens, immigrant and native-born children alike, could be socialized and educated together on the tenets of democracy.

Keep in mind that in 1918 another great wave of immigration was under way, World War I was raging, women could not vote, many immigrant groups were treated as less than human and discriminated against (e.g., Italians and other southern Europeans), and still less than 5 percent of children graduated from high school and many did not attend school past grade 8. There were concerns that democracy might not be the best form of government.

The members of the Commission recognized the importance of having more students enter and stay in high school, and they called for a massive reform of the secondary school curriculum. The focus changed from a mechanistic, one-size-fits-all approach to a program connected to the students through a curriculum based on social problem solving, democracy, and authentic learning of skills and knowledge students would need to become contributing members of their community, culture, and the larger society. The focus was to develop the individual to his/her maximum potential so that he/she will forward his/her culture, improve his community, and contribute to his country.

We see the *Cardinal Principles of Secondary Education* as education's Declaration of Independence from the ideas of an elitist, dual system, and it sent shock waves through the establishment. The authors of the *Cardinal Principles* called for educating all children through high school in the same system in an untracked, yet differentiated, curricular program. All students would participate in a curriculum that included the fundamental processes (traditional subject matter).

But the *Principles* went beyond the basics and proposed a "common core" based on social problem solving, the problems of democracy. The problems of society would form the backbone of the common core and all students would participate during all four years of high school.

Knowing that many students would not finish high school, the curriculum was sequenced so that those students who completed at least grade 10 would leave with basic academic content, an exploration of the problems of society, and a basic foundation in the role of a participative citizen. Students who stayed in school beyond grade 10 would have the chance to access various curricular programs aimed at college preparation or career specializations.

The *Principles* called for the operationalization of helping students work for the greater good through the fusion of what we would call "white"- and "blue"-collar career education with service learning. The authors envisioned a secondary school program where students take part in career education inside and outside the schoolhouse with an emphasis on developing self, culture, community, and country.

For example, a specialized set of electives in home economics were proposed for girls. The Commission laid out ideas for a high school curriculum known as Worthy Home Membership that recognized women as the backbone of democracy because women had the responsibility to raise the next generation of citizens. The Commission members believed that democracy started in the home and extended to the community. Therefore, women deserved the opportunity to access a specialized curriculum.

The *Cardinal Principles* were truly futuristic in thinking about the role and importance of women in a democratic society. The *Principles* placed women in a central role in the republic during a time when women could not even vote. The idea of the woman as the head of the household and matriarch of the community with primary responsibility for rearing the next generation of citizens continued another 50 years until the late 1960s and the advent of the modern women's liberation movement. The Commission identified the importance of women to the democracy.

The document was a democratic proposal, and it helped the suffrage movement succeed and influenced the Civil Rights movement (D. Tanner, personal communication, May 2011). It is beyond the scope of our work here to spend more time on the *Principles*. We encourage readers to examine the actual document and come to know the *Principles*.

We owe a debt of gratitude to the authors of *Cardinal Principles*, for they illuminated an education program for secondary school children drawn from Jefferson's ideas that every citizen should possess the skills and information necessary to conduct his own business matters and be able to understand his/her role and responsibility as a productive citizen to his family, community, and country (Jefferson, 1818).

Jefferson threw down the challenge to future generations and almost exactly a century later, the *Cardinal Principles of Secondary Education* provided a blueprint for a system to realize Jefferson's, Carter's, Mann's, and Barnard's visions. The practices of differentiated instruction, differentiated curriculum, cocurricular activities, enrichment courses, exploratory electives, and specialized course sequences within one comprehensive high school were just some of the things that came out of the *Principles* and survive today in some places.

The Principles Come Alive

The *Cardinal Principles* were futuristic in their specific ideas about socializing all peoples into the democracy on a level playing field, but they were more about ideas and less about actions. The 1920s through 1940s saw an explosion of progressive/experimentalist experiments and the eventual operationalization of the *Cardinal Principles*.

Thorndike's initial study (1901), and then later his 1924 landmark study with 8,564 children, once and for all crushed the myth of mental discipline when his results demonstrated that there was not a hierarchy of secondary school subjects, and no one subject was superior to another when it came to overall growth in intelligence. Thorndike's studies exposed the fundamental flaws in the Committee of Ten's recommendations for one set program of studies in high school.

Unfortunately, it appears as if many of the state commissioners of education and various education bureaucrats in the United States either don't remember Thorndike or did not read the study. This is evidenced by the majority of education bureaucrats who jumped on the bandwagon of the American Diploma Project (ADP) vended by Achieve, Inc. (2008) and now blindly support the Common Core State Standards (CCSS) initiative.

The ADP and CCSS are simply a reincarnation of an educationally bankrupt idea that was empirically destroyed over 85 years ago, yet due to a lack of understanding of their own history, education leaders are willing to follow business interests over the cliff of botched reforms again. Thorndike's studies added credence to the *Cardinal Principles'* idea of a large macrocurriculum that allowed students to take multiple paths through high school while having all the paths embedded in authentic problem solving and socially conscious studies that connected to the experiences of students and larger society.

Wrightstone (1935) and Wrightstone, Rechetnick, McCall, and Loftus (1939) conducted a series of studies to determine the effects of an activity curriculum on student achievement and social dispositions of students in the New York City public schools. Elementary school students in grades 4 through 6 in 69 schools across the city were placed in experimental and control groups.

The sample of matched-pairs students included 32 control classes and 32 experimental classes. The final sample of students matched for comparison purposes was approximately 9,000. Students were tested prior to the experiment and found to be similar in academic achievement and social dispositions. The control group students had the advantage in intelligence by the equivalent of one month of schooling.

The posttest results indicated that the students who engaged in the activity-based curriculum demonstrated more academic and affective growth than students in a traditional program. Students were assessed in the following areas: (a) comprehensive achievement in reading and mathematics, (b) cooperation activities, (c) experimental activities that require creation or construction of new ideas, and (d) critical activities such as critique, persuasion, or defending points of view.

The posttest results also showed superior gains in leadership activities, self-initiated activities, and work spirit activities. Students in the activity curriculum classrooms outscored their peers on all assessments except the recitations. The effect size difference between the academic achievements on the comprehensive assessment was 0.21, favoring the activity group. The results demonstrated the efficacy of a non-standardized curriculum to improve student achievement.

Jersild, Thorndike, and Goldman (1939; 1941) reported on the results of what came to be known as the New York City experiment that included 75,000 elementary school students. Once again the students involved in an activity-based curriculum outperformed their peers from traditional college preparatory programs on measures of academic and affective growth.

These studies demonstrated the power of the ideas communicated in the *Cardinal Principles of Secondary Education* and suggested that the ideas can be applied to elementary and secondary education. However, these studies paled in comparison to what is still considered "the" landmark study in education: the Eight-Year Study, which we will discuss later in the chapter.

The Educational Policies Commission (EPC) emerged in 1938 with a report that set forth five "ideals" (EPC, 1938) that schools should seek to foster in students: (a) humanitarianism; (b) understanding and respect for the rights of other peoples; (c) civic participation in decision making; (d) methods of solving local, national, and international disputes that arrive at peaceful resolutions; and (e) the ability to evaluate the effectiveness of domestic and foreign policies in helping people progress in society (pp. 7–9).

Although the members of the EPC did not recommend a unitary system overtly in the 1938 report, one can infer that the "ideals" were not reserved only for a ruling class and that instead all children should experience the type of education that would help to achieve them. The connection between the EPC's ideals and the *Cardinal Principles* is clear. Another clue that the members of the EPC were not proposing a dual system was in the Commission's admonition regarding standardized testing.

Testing as a way of sorting students was gaining popularity, born out of the U.S. Army's use of the Alpha Test to select officer candidates during World War I. The Commission communicated clearly that standardized tests were limited in their ability and scope of measuring student achievement and the myopic focus on measuring isolated bits of information. It is interesting that more than 70 years later our education leaders and policy makers have yet to understand the Commission's warnings and recommendations.

The EPC released several other reports in the following years (1944 and 1952) that would add to their initial ideas. The report known as *Education for ALL America's Youth* proposed an eight-year curriculum beginning in grade 7 and extending into grade 14. This proposal, also known as the 2X2 model, created a bridge from the high school to a career or postsecondary schooling. Although the model never gained universal support, aspects of the idea remain today in some schools that offer work-study, apprenticeship, and dual-credit college enrollment programs.

The Eight-Year Study

If the *Cardinal Principles of Secondary Education* was education's Declaration of Independence from the dual system, then the Eight-Year Study (Aikin, 1942) provided a road map to achieve independence. The study grew out of the progressive/experimentalist philosophy and operationalized the *Cardinal Principles*. It included thirty high schools/districts from across the country. Troubled by the stranglehold that college admissions had on the high school curriculum, some university professors and the educators from the thirty schools sought a new way, a democratic way, to achieve excellence for all students, not just those who intended to go to college.

The participants set out to design and implement secondary school programs that brought the *Cardinal Principles* to life. They worked with hundreds of colleges and received agreements that their students would not be subject to traditional standardized test–driven entrance criteria if the personnel from the thirty schools could demonstrate that their students were just as well prepared as students coming from traditional high schools. Thus, they were freed from their curricular chains.

The curricular programs of the thirty schools were not standardized. In fact, they were synthesized from the recommendations of the *Cardinal Principles*, progressive/experimentalist philosophy, and research of the time on the nature of the learner, human development, and the nature of knowledge, as well as influence from social forces, including democratic ideals. The program at each school was unique yet focused on a paradigm of curriculum and instruction based on an understanding that had five overriding principles.

The first principle was that the learner is an active constructor of meaning who brings prior knowledge and experience to the classroom, and school policies and practices should capitalize on those experiences. Second, knowledge is organized as a fusion of discipline-centered subject matter and personal/societal experiences, connecting the content to students through authentic social problem-solving situations that examined issues facing democracy. Third, student social and cognitive development is ongoing and occurs in stages, not at finite points in time like the end of grade 9.

Democracy itself was the fourth principle. Democracy is a strong cultural force that cannot be ignored, and as such, any initiative that is pushed from the top down is likely not to achieve its stated goals because it violates cultural norms of democratic participation and decision making. Equity was the final principle. Equity is the idea that getting what one needs (diversification of curriculum) and not the same as everyone else (standardization of curriculum) should be a driving force in education.

Students in the thirty schools pursued diverse interests within a large macrocurriculum that provided a common core of study on the challenges facing the democracy, instruction in the basic academic subjects, and a large set of electives to allow for career specialization, exploration, and enrichment. The lack of standardization and the nonfocus on solely testing recall information produced superior results.

Ralph Tyler headed the evaluation of the project. The results suggested that when matched with similar students from traditional high schools, the students from the 30 schools outperformed their peers on all measures of academic achievement, including standardized tests. The students from the thirty schools achieved higher college grade-point averages and demonstrated better problem-solving skills and civic-minded behaviors among other things. The only academic area that they did not statistically significantly outperform their peers was in foreign language (Aikin, 1942).

The results from the Eight-Year Study demonstrated that public secondary schools can educate all students together; differentiate curriculum and instruction to meet their unique needs; diversify course offerings; operate in truly nonstandardized democratic ways in which teachers, administrators, and university professors work together to solve problems; produce better results; and ultimately fill the role proposed by Jefferson and the other historic defenders of a democratic, classless education system.

In the end it was diversification, guided by a paradigm of curriculum and instruction based on a progressive philosophy informed by professional judgment and research, that trumped standardization and a one-size-fits-all mentality of elitist education. Once again, it is not our objective to write the definitive narrative of the Eight-Year Study. Others have already done that well (e.g., Kridel & Bullough, 2007). We recommend those interested people read the study for themselves.

We might add that the Eight-Year Study was published just as World War II was under way, and the study of the problems that faced democracy was not a priority. Thus, its overall effect on education policy after World War II was rather diminished. Keep in mind that the political climate at the time was not kind to school curriculum programs that taught students to question democracy or to study the problems of a democracy. The rise of Russia and then China led to curricular retrenchment in the basics and away from problem-based learning.

Progressive/experimentalist education policy reforms as a whole, and their curricular programs, were falling out of favor. Curriculum materials and supporting resources, such as the *Building America* series of problem-based units, were under attack by the "conservative press and ultra right-wing groups" (Tanner, 1991, p. 45) as being sympathetic to communism. The *Building America* series was used by many schools that engaged in socially conscious, problem-based curricula work. In fact, in 1945, the year that regressive, antiexperimental/antiprogressive attacks began in earnest, the series sold 1 million copies per monthly issue (Tanner, 1991).

By 1948, publication stopped due to the increasing false allegations that members of the *Building America* editorial board members were communist sympathizers. Many school boards across the country removed the books from school shelves and destroyed them. The questioning of democracy and a study of its problems was not tolerated in the post–World War II era.

Although World War II, the rise of communism and socialism, and an American inferiority complex put an end to the large-scale progressive/experimentalist practices at the thirty schools and in education policy across the country, the contribution of those practices to demonstrating the power of the free public school system to provide a quality education cannot be dismissed. Whereas some might cast aside the historical research we provided as being out of date or no longer relevant, we reply by asking: Are Newton's laws out of date, are Galileo's discoveries no longer relevant, or is the discovery that aspirin helps to ease some types of pain now irrelevant because those experiments and discoveries took place some time ago?

The hamster wheel of education reform continues to turn because in some cases its leaders don't recognize when someone has gotten off and blazed a new direction. We find it interesting that in a profession of education, anti-intellectualism and historical laziness seem to pervade. We ask our readers to reacquaint themselves with education's rich history and research in an attempt to once again reestablish the role and responsibility of public education as a unitary system devoted to leveling the playing field within a truly participative democracy.

EFFICIENCY: EDUCATION'S OTHER REFORM

Although education reform based on democratic ideals and a unitary conception of public education gained strength during the turn of the twentieth century up through World War II, there was another reform movement under way, perhaps even stronger in its intoxicating appeal. This reform was to become known as the scientific management or the efficiency movement (Taylor, 1947). The efficiency movement in education was less concerned with equity, liberty and justice for all, and democratic ideals and more concerned with squeezing every ounce of perceived waste out of the system, at a cost to effectiveness.

The efficiency movement propelled the popularity of monitorial instruction and the Gary Plan, also known as platoon schools. The Gary Plan, named after a school structure used in Gary, Indiana, was developed by William Wirt in 1908 after he became superintendent (Callahan, 1962). Wirt proposed that classrooms should not be empty during the school day, because that was an indication of waste.

There was much made of school buildings not being used both night and day nor all year around at that time. Wirt realized that if schools became departmentalized by academic subject, then all the students could move from room to room throughout the day and homerooms and specialty rooms could also be in use due to the rotating system. No longer was a room only for homeroom activities. With departmentalized instruction, the homeroom could become the math room for some additional periods during the day followed by an English room, followed by a foreign language room.

The Gary Plan caught on, and by 1925 the plan was in use in 632 schools in 126 cities (Callahan, 1962, p. 129). Although the plan sounds commonsensical today, its focus was not on education as much as it was on economization. For example, the idea was brought to the elementary-school level in New York City without the research to support its use at that level. It was also used to develop double and triple school sessions so that the school plant was in constant use or as close to 100 percent utilization as possible.

Keep in mind that triple sessions means students are physically at school at night. The disruption to the family structure, daily student routines, and lack of research did not deter the efficiency gurus and the wannabe business-captain superintendents from climbing aboard the efficiency train. Callahan (1962) noted that observers of the platoon school commented that students looked like machines marching in line and that the schools exhibited a hyper focus on the number of students being educated within the shortest number of hours. Schooling was done "to" those students, and not "with" or "for" the students.

Although other proposals to keep portions of the platoon school idea emerged during the time period, those that did not provide the same level of facility usage and cost efficiency, no matter how much research supported the alternative ideas, did not succeed. This added further confirmation to the detractors of the platoon school plan that it was all about economics and not about education.

Of course the Gary Plan and platoon schools were adopted more frequently in the cities where more diverse and poorer students attended school. We say of course because it seems once again that those in power prescribe a less democratic system for those who come to school with less. The support for a dual system of education, albeit perhaps on economic terms, was alive and well through the operationalization of the efficiency movement.

Remember, efficiency is not the same as effectiveness, and effectiveness is not always efficient. Efficiency is concerned with maximizing profit at all costs, as we have painfully witnessed and experienced as a result of the hyper profit-efficiency movement currently running Wall Street and part of the charter school movement. Also remember that Frederick Taylor's ideas of efficiency and scientific management were created in the steel mills focused on the shoveling of coal and developing iron, inanimate objects. School leaders work with children, human beings.

POINTS TO REMEMBER

There is no evidence that the efficiency movement of the late 1800s and early 1900s improved education; in fact, evidence exists that the opposite was true. Consider that the public high school graduation rate in 1918, well into the efficiency movement, was about 5 percent.

The first 200 years of public school development in the United States was marked by an ongoing rivalry between proponents of a dual system and those who supported a unitary, democratic system of public education for all students. We are sure you can see the rivalry continue today if you look below the surface of today's reform movement.

A LOOK AHEAD

The next chapter transitions from education's distant past and brings us into the modern reform era with Sputnik and *A Nation at Risk*, and it presents our critical analyses of these reform drivers. The analyses derive from empirical evidence and other facts. As we will argue with evidence, the education reform sun does not revolve around the Earth. Regardless of ideology, we believe fact should trump fiction when it comes to social policy making.

REFERENCES

Achieve, Inc. (2008). Closing the expectations gap. Author. Retrieved from www.achieve.org/files/50-state-2008-final02-25-08.pdf.

Aikin, W. M. (1942). *The Story of the Eight-Year Study*. New York: Harper.

Callahan, R. E. (1962). *The Cult of Efficiency*. Chicago: The University of Chicago Press.

Campbell, J. K. (1967). *Colonel Parker: The Children's Crusader*. New York: Teachers College Press.

Commission on the Reorganization of Secondary Education. (1918). *Cardinal Principles of Secondary Education*. Washington, DC: U.S. Bureau of Education, Bulletin No. 35.

Dewey, J. (1897). My Pedagogic Creed. *School Journal* 54: 77–80.

Dewey, J. (1899). *School and Society*. Chicago: University of Chicago. Original publication date.

Dewey, J. (1916). *Democracy and Education*. New York: Macmillan.

Education Policies Commission. (1938). The purposes of education in American democracy. Washington, DC: National Education Association of the United States and the American Association of School Administrators.

Education Policies Commission. (1944). Education for ALL American youth. Washington, DC: National Education Association.

Education Policies Commission. (1952). Education for ALL American youth: A further look. Washington, D.C.: National Education Association.

Freier, P. (2000). *Pedagogy of the Oppressed: 30th Anniversary Edition*. New York: Continuum.

Jefferson, T. (1818). Report of the commissioners appointed to fix the site of the university of Virginia. In Roy J. Honeywell, 1964. *The Educational Works of Thomas Jefferson*. New York: Russell and Russell; Appendix J.

Jersild, A. T., Thorndike, R. L. & Goldman, B. (1939). An Evaluation of Aspects of the Activity Program in New York City Elementary Schools. *Journal of Experimental Education* 8: 166–207.

Jersild, A. T., Thorndike, R. L. & Goldman, B. (1941). A Further Comparison of Pupils in "Activity" and "Non-Activity" Schools. *Journal of Experimental Education* 9: 307–309.

Jewett, T. O. (1997). Thomas Jefferson and the Purposes of Education. *The Educational Forum* 61: 110–113.

Kridel, C. & Bullough, R. V. Jr. (2007.) *Stories of the Eight-Year Study: Reexamining Secondary Education in America*. Albany: State University Press of New York.

Mann, H. (1848). *Twelfth annual report of the board of education together with the twelfth annual report of the secretary of the board*. Boston, Massachusetts: Dutton and Wentworth State Printers.

National Education Association of the United States, Committee of Ten on Secondary School Studies. (1893). Report of the Committee of Ten on Secondary School Studies; With the Reports of the Conferences Arranged by the Committee. Imprint New York, Published for the National Education Association, by the American Book Co., 1984.

Padover, S. K. (1939). *Thomas Jefferson on Democracy*. New York: Appleton-Century Company, Inc.

Rayman, R. (1981). Joseph Lancaster's Monitorial System of Education and American Indian Education. *History of Education Quarterly* 21(4): 395–409.

Tanner, D. (1991). *Crusade for Democracy: Progressive Education at the Crossroads*. Albany: State University of New York Press.

Tanner, D. & Tanner, L. (2007). *Curriculum Development: Theory into Practice*. New York: Allyn & Bacon.

Taylor, F. W. (1947). *Scientific Management*. New York: Harper and Brothers.

Thorndike, E. L. (1924). Mental Discipline in High School Studies. *Journal of Educational Psychology* 15: 1–22, 98.

Thorndike, E. L. & Woodworth, R. S. (1901). The Influence of Improvement in One Mental Function upon Efficiency of Other Functions. *Psychological Review* 8: 247–261, 384–395, 553–564.

Williams, F. D. (1989). *The Northwest Ordinance: Essays on Its Formulation, Provisions, and Legacy*. East Lansing: Michigan State University Press.

Wrightstone, J. W. (1935). *Appraisal of Newer Practices in Selected Public Schools*. New York: Teachers College Press.

Wrightstone, J. W., Rechetnick, J., McCall, W. A. & Loftus, J. J. (1939). Measuring Social Performance Factors in Activity Control Schools of New York City. *Teachers College Record* 40(5): 423–432.

TWO

The Education Reform King with a Styrofoam Crown

By and large, the American public believes from firsthand experience that the nation's public schools provide students with the knowledge, skills, and competencies they need to be successful (Bushaw & McNee, 2009). They believe in the Jeffersonian view of a democratic, unitary system of public education. For millions of individuals, the public schools provided the opportunities that allowed them to realize their own "American dream."

Many people believe that individual success comes with education, and from an economic standpoint, this is often true (Bushaw & McNee, 2009). As the U.S. Bureau of the Census reported, individual incomes are highly correlated with years of formal education (see U.S. Census Bureau, 2009). To be certain, there are unemployed college graduates, but education achievement is one path out of poverty for some in America.

It's also true the "dream" is not uniformly achieved. Not all individuals in our society profit equally from education. The reasons vary, from socioeconomic factors to racial and ethnic inequalities and biases (Murray, 1999). But those lucky enough to have choices would choose a good education and the basic opportunities it affords.

Why then is the American public school system the subject of so much criticism and many attempts to pervert the public unitary system into a dual system that provides quality education to some and a narrow, mechanistic education to others? Two reasons are simply the colossal size and scope of America's public education system and the massive amount of public money contained within that system.

In this chapter we critically deconstruct one of the most cited political events to influence school reform along with one of the most influential federal reports. Our analyses reveal that (a) things are often not as dire as

19

dual-system proponents described them when it comes to public education and (b) one should not believe everything that is printed about public education being in crisis.

SPUTNIK: THE REIGNING KING

In the category of *events make history*: October 4, 1957, was marked by the shocking announcement from Moscow, Russia, that the Soviets had successfully launched their Sputnik space satellite. The shock waves rocked the free world. The Soviets launched more than a satellite on October 4, 1957. They helped launch the wave of modern school reforms that haunt us still today.

Unfortunately no one stopped to realize that America could have launched a satellite many months earlier than the Soviets. Some Americans still accept that the launch of Sputnik signaled that the American public education system was inadequate. Anecdotally, many of our education leadership students also think that, as do policy makers. They, like many other citizens, fail to look below the surface and critique the conventional wisdom. Our biases and critical social theory lens require us to examine this important event and to be skeptical.

American presidents since Eisenhower and/or their secretaries of education have used Sputnik, the reigning king of the modern school reform movement, as an instrument of fear or as a historical reminder of policy makers' belief that education is a national security priority, to push education reforms. The use of Sputnik to legitimize policy actions continues even today. President Obama stated (2009), "When the Soviet Union launched Sputnik a little more than a half century ago, Americans were stunned. The Russians had beaten us to space." Obama's secretary of education Arne Duncan (2009) used Sputnik to advance his Race to the Top (RTTT) initiative.

> In 1957, the Soviet Union launched Sputnik. They showed the world that they were leading the space race. President Eisenhower and Congress responded by establishing NASA. But they also funded efforts to create new curriculum and programs to advance mathematics and science in our schools. They understood that education would help us win the Space Race—and any other race.

Unfortunately President Obama and his education secretary continue to perpetuate the mythology of education crisis with their frequent calls for a "Sputnik moment" in education. It seems that when a high-ranking bureaucrat wants to push an initiative, they wheel out Sputnik.

Former U.S. Secretary of Education Rod Paige used Sputnik to support the 2003 Mathematics and Science Initiative:

When the federal government last launched a major initiative promoting mathematics and science education after *Sputnik*, within 12 years, America had upgraded mathematics and science education, launched satellites, and seen its astronauts orbit the Earth and land on the Moon.

President Bill Clinton's secretary of education Richard Riley (1995) used Sputnik to justify further federal involvement in education as part of the America 2000 legislation:

When the Russians woke us up by flying Sputnik over our heads late at night—a few of you may remember that experience—Congress passed the 1958 National Defense Education Act, which sent millions of Americans to college and educated a generation of scientists who helped us to win the Cold War.

Ronald Reagan used Sputnik as a propaganda tool in 1982 to support his plan to give tax credits for parents to send their students to private schools (*Time* magazine, 1982). Is this crowning of Sputnik as the king of modern school reform justified? Did American public education let down the country and compromise national security? Not so fast.

A review of some memos and communications during the Eisenhower administration tell another story of Sputnik. Sputnik became a manufactured crisis, to borrow a term by Berliner and Biddle (1995). In reality Sputnik is just a vagabond king wearing a Styrofoam crown (Bon Jovi & Sambora, 1995). What follows is a review of presidential memos and speeches that expose the use of Sputnik as a myth, built on fear and lies, to manufacture the need for reform. We propose that the use of Sputnik in this way is misguided and intellectually weak.

Eisenhower Speaks

President Eisenhower held a meeting with his top staff on October 8, 1957 to discuss the launch of Sputnik. Declassified memos indicate that Eisenhower was not overly upset or worried about the situation. In fact, the quality of the U.S. education system was not a concern of Eisenhower's. According to the then Deputy Secretary of Defense Quarles, who was present at the October 8 meeting, "the Redstone [military rocket] had it been used could have orbited a satellite a year or more ago" (Goodpaster, 1957a, p. 1).

President Eisenhower did not want to be the first into space because of fears of igniting a third world war with the Soviets. The president was pleased when Sputnik launched first because to him, the Soviets opened up space for the United States. He stated during the October 8 meeting that the Russians "have done us a good turn unintentionally in establishing the concept of internationalizing space" (Goodpaster, 1957a, p. 2).

At the 339th meeting of the National Security Council on October 10, 1957, six days after the launch, Secretary Quarles stated, "Our Government had never regarded this program as including as a major objective that the United States should launch an earth satellite first, though, of course, we have always been aware of the cold war implications of the launching of the first earth satellite" (Gleason, 1957, p. 3).

As best can be determined through access to declassified documents found in the U.S. National Archives and the Eisenhower Library, the idea that U.S. schooling was inferior first came from propaganda put out by Nikita Khrushchev and the Chinese communist government immediately following the launch. The Soviets and Chinese seized upon the Sputnik launch to create their own propaganda offensive in an attempt to show the world that communism was superior to Western-style governments.

Keep in mind that at the time, the Soviets were expanding their communist bloc and looking for any positive press to help them overcome the unsavory picture being painted of the Iron Curtain. Likewise, the Chinese communists were under constant pressure to control their large empire and needed positive propaganda to support their struggling government.

It wasn't until an October 15, 1957, meeting between the president and several scientific advisors that education began to enter into the conversation, and only casually as a way to persuade Congress and the American public to support more funding for basic and specialized scientific research, not K-12 science education. Dr. I. I. Rabi told the president, " . . . we can now see some advantages [scientific] on our part. However, the Soviets picked up tremendous momentum . . . " (Goodpaster, 1957b, p. 2). Dr. E. H. Land stated that the scientific community needed the president's support to bring more of a focus to science. He said, "At this time scientists feel themselves isolated and alone, but all of this could change" (Goodpaster, 1957b, p. 2).

The scientists themselves began to create lore of Russian superiority in science education. That lore would fan the flames of attacks on public schools for years to come. Dr. E. H. Land told the president, "They [the Soviets] regard science both as an essential tool and a way of life. They are teaching their young people to enjoy science" (Goodpaster, 1957b, p. 2).

Dr. Land went on to accurately portray the tenor of the times and the rising role of consumption in the United States as it influenced science and discovery during those years leading up to Sputnik. "Curiously, in the United States, we are not now great builders for the future, but are rather stressing production in great quantities of things we already achieved" (p. 2).

To his credit, Eisenhower pushed back against the idea that the Soviets were superior in science education. Eisenhower said it was his understanding that the Soviets "followed the practice of picking out the best minds and ruthlessly spurning the rest" (Goodpaster, 1957b, p. 2). It seems as if Eisenhower understood the need for a democratic, unitary system that attempted to provide all students with quality education opportunities. But Eisenhower did see the need for a "coordinated effort" on the issue of funding for science research and stated that he was in favor of trying to "create a spirit, an attitude toward science similar to that held toward various kinds of athletics in his youth" (Goodpaster, 1957b, p. 2).

It was the science community that saw the potential of attaching basic education to the Sputnik issue as a way to mobilize support for more funding in the research labs and universities. Eisenhower agreed and stated that ". . . now is a good time to try such a thing. People are alarmed and thinking about science, and perhaps this alarm could be turned to a constructive result" (p. 2).

Remember that the federal government had very little influence on the K-12 curriculum at that time and the idea of federal incursions into the classrooms was not welcomed. The researchers, Congress, and to some extent the president saw Sputnik not as an education crisis, but as an opportunity to push federal money into education and research.

A little more than one month after the launch of Sputnik the president made a speech on November 7, 1957, about science and national security to announce a series of actions he was prepared to take. Education was not mentioned in that speech. It wasn't until November 13, 1957, approximately six weeks following the launch of Sputnik, that Eisenhower brought education to the forefront. This is perhaps the speech that created the myth of U.S. public education inferiority that would haunt educators until this day.

In his speech Eisenhower began to paint the picture of a superior Soviet education system and of the United States falling behind educationally. Several statements are quite poignant. Eisenhower (1957) stated, "We know of their rigorous educational system and their technological achievements." (Even though one month earlier he rebuked one of the researchers who made that comment in his office.)

Eisenhower then made the direct connection between the support for research wanted by the scientists and weaving in their idea to link this to the general public through a connection with basic education. "Time is a big factor in two longer-term problems: strengthening our scientific education and our basic research." At this point, the reader should keep in mind that we were the country that invented the atomic bomb before anyone else. Did our scientific education and basic research degenerate to a place so low that in the span of just 12 years Russia could be superior in science education?

Eisenhower went on to make an amazing claim during the speech: "As you do this, my friends, remember that when a Russian graduates from high school he has had five years of physics, four years of chemistry, one year of astronomy, five years of biology, ten years of mathematics through trigonometry, and five years of a foreign language."

To our knowledge, no nation on the planet graduates even a majority, let alone "all" of its students from high school having taken all of those courses, and in fact it was not true then. Eisenhower asked that the public ". . . scrutinize your school's curriculum and standards. Then decide for yourselves whether they meet the stern demands of the era we are entering." He in fact helped, maybe unwittingly, start the fears, myths, and lies about America's public schools. This was the flashpoint, the modern dual-system reformer's *Book of Genesis*.

Then Eisenhower laid out what now appears to be the road map for modern day "reform" efforts. "We should, among other things, have a system of nation-wide testing of high school students; a system of incentives for high aptitude students to pursue scientific or professional studies; a program to stimulate good-quality teaching of mathematics and science; provision of more laboratory facilities; and measures, including fellowships, to increase the output of qualified teachers."

One can see Sputnik's mutated spawn—the No Child Left Behind Act, Common Core State Standards, and National Standardized Testing— waiting in the wings of that speech. Eisenhower legitimized Sputnik as the symbol of American education's inferiority when in fact, the United States had technological superiority over the Soviets at that time and never lost it. The king was crowned, and so it began.

CRISIS MENTALITY

The Soviets' launch of Sputnik created an *educational crisis* in the United States; at least that is what public school critics claimed. Bureaucrats in Washington, D.C., quickly set out to fix our schools. School critics and highly paid lobbyists stumbled around with absolutely positive "fixes" for the schools. This was all done without anyone stopping to ask, "What actually needs fixing?" What evidence is there to demonstrate the schools are actually broken?

Attempts to reform our state and national education systems are often akin to calling a plumber, saying "Fix the plumbing," and walking out. At the end of the day, the plumber is still in the basement trying to figure out what needs fixing.

National Defense Education Act

Using the crisis momentum created by the Soviets' launch of Sputnik and a speech given by President Eisenhower on November 13, 1957, the U.S. Congress responded with the now famous National Defense Education Act (NDEA). The NDEA provided the public schools and research universities with hundreds of millions of dollars to "catch up," although the United States was never behind. In September 1958, eleven months after the launch of Sputnik I, the National Defense Education Act was signed by President Eisenhower.

The enabling clause states that the NDEA was designed "to strengthen the national defense and to encourage and assist in the expansion and improvement of educational programs to meet critical national needs . . . " (NDEA, U.S. Statutes at Large, 1958). The stated motive was "to meet critical national needs," not to meet school needs or the needs of children or young adolescents.

The NDEA was administered through the U.S. Office of Education. However, it must be noted that the NDEA was not a federal educational program, per se, but rather federally supported state programs in eight areas: (1) college and university student loans; (2) grants to states and loans to nonprofit private schools for purchase of equipment and improvement of state supervision to strengthen elementary and secondary instruction in science, mathematics, and modern foreign languages; (3) graduate study fellowships; (4) grants to states and contractual arrangements with institutions of higher learning to strengthen guidance counseling and testing in secondary schools, and to establish institutes for secondary school guidance and counseling personnel; (5) modern foreign language institutes for elementary and secondary school language teachers, and language area study centers for work in rarely taught modern languages, and for the conduct of research; (6) research and experimentation in more effective use of modern communications media for educational purposes; (7) grants to states for development of area vocational education programs in scientific or technical fields; and (8) grants to states to improve statistical services of state educational agencies.

The federal legislation simply identified the areas to be funded, whereas states, local agencies, and universities had great leeway in addressing the federal needs. The NDEA was a federal policy of accommodation, not control or coercion. The goal was to provide fiscal aid, input aid, for pressing national problems.

The NDEA was not critical of the schools. NDEA illustrates how our governmental leaders and policy makers react to any perceived crisis, even when there is no crisis, as was known at the time. The mishandling of the Sputnik event created an atmosphere of national "soul searching."

Obviously, there were unlisted problems in our schools that appeared to impact our national security, like segregation. NDEA did not fix that, but the legislation did give policy makers something to take back to their constituents and say, "See, I am doing something . . . now can you vote for me again." In the eyes of a policy maker, fixing a perceived crisis is just as good as fixing a real crisis. So, to fix that perceived weakness and to show the public that our nation would respond to any challenge, the NDEA was passed.

Further, NDEA was one of the first broadly supported federal initiatives to aid public education. It set the tone for what was to come. Note carefully that when the NDEA was proposed, no one asked: "Did Russian schoolkids build Sputnik?" Nevertheless, blame for Sputnik being launched before an American satellite was eventually laid at the feet of the American public school employees and the system at large.

The method of introducing "reform" using a national and/or international crisis while the populace is in a state of shock continues today, as seen in the response to Hurricane Katrina and even the economic crisis of 2008 (Klein, 2008).

SCHOOLS AND POLITICS

The programs and policies implemented immediately following Sputnik represented a change in federal involvement and reach into public education. As we uncovered in the declassified memos, federal legislators sought ways to inject federal dollars and some influence into the large, decentralized public school system, that up until Sputnik, was resistant to federal incursions into the locally controlled system.

Like most things associated with federal dollars, politics "came a-calling" to the schoolhouse following the passage of the NDEA in 1958 and has since continued unabated. Traditionally, educators feared politics. The misconceptions involved in this attitude are amplified by the following excerpt taken from the January 1963 *Carnegie Corporation of New York Quarterly.*

> Public education is paid for by public funds, and public funds are raised, and allocated, through the political process . . . In short, the political forum is where the citizenry fights about the things it cares about; it is where the public assigns priorities and establishes its values in rank order.
>
> Not everyone comprehends this trading out of interests in the political market place. This is one reason why many political decisions do not in fact reflect accurately the most widely held public values but do often reflect those of "interests" which understand the political process very well indeed. In these cases, where does the fault lie except with those who are either too lazy or too naïve to press the case effectively for their own "interests"?
>
> For the basic importance of the inseparability of politics and education is not the fact that public money supports public education but what that fact represents: that the education of its youth is a primary interest of the nation. And the nation has many legitimate concerns—for defense, health, highways, and welfare, as well as education. The equitable allocation of resources in support of these interests is an extraordinarily intricate—and political—"business." (p. 1, reprinted with permission)

Mathews & McAfee (2003) make a compelling case for understanding the public's role in policy making through the political arena. They explore the links between communities and their schools. Public schools grew in the United States because there was a strong communal spirit working in concert to create and support them. One of the key points is that there is need for deliberation in public decision making. Through constructive deliberation the citizens in a community make education (and other government functions) more effective.

We would parenthetically underscore the need for public deliberation concerning school reform. During the late 1980s and early 1990s, Governor Booth Gardner of Washington State held a series of statewide "Town Meetings" to sell his education reform package. Not one of these meetings resulted in the public endorsing his plans, but he went ahead anyway. This is a case study of not deliberating with the public but "telling them." We will revisit the consequences of this reform model.

Foundations have played a very significant role in the field of education, and these fine institutions are not above politics. In "War of Ideas," Andrew Rich (2005) presented a thoughtful analysis of the role that foundations play in school reform. He observed that while liberal think tanks and foundations spend more money in supporting their agenda, the conservative ones spend less and are more effective. This might be because conservatives, as a group, do not rely on science and evidence and are more apt to go along with the group.

The effectiveness of conservative institutions also comes from the fact that they deliberately focus on shaping public policy—making them overtly political bodies. Rich illustrates how the conservative foundations influence public policy with strong organizations that support their causes, which include school reform policies that provide for school choice.

As we will see in later chapters, choice is a preferred mechanism for a dual system to expand. George Lakoff (2004) commented that conservative and Republican-oriented think tanks convert their research into what might be labeled two-word philosophies: "Family Values," "School Reform," "School Accountability," or "School Choice." All of these slogans carry philosophical connotations far beyond the simple words involved, and all appeal for political support.

ANOTHER KING COMES CALLING

In April 1983, the Republican administration controlled the U.S. Department of Education and assembled the National Commission on Excellence in Education (NCEE, 1983), a "blue ribbon panel" with the obviously unannounced purpose of debasing the public schools. The Reagan administration used the report as one piece of a total strategy to lay the groundwork for an unsuccessful attempt to legislate school vouchers and tax credits for parents who sent their children to private schools.

The idea of vilifying public schools as a way to introduce vouchers, choice, privatization, and other neoliberal free-market concepts would continue, but *Risk* demonstrated the power of manufacturing an education crisis through a federal report. In *A Nation at Risk: The Imperative for Educational Reform,* the commission members claimed to illustrate the gravity of the situation with the following assertion. "If an unfriendly foreign power had attempted to impose on America the mediocre instructional performance that exists today, we might well have viewed it as an act of war."

David Berliner and Bruce Biddle (1995) observed that using a war metaphor intentionally created a national security crisis. The *Risk* report sent shock waves through the education establishment and gave the would-be school reformers the shot in the arm they had been lacking since King Sputnik arrived on the scene. The war metaphor was nonsensical rhetoric, but it worked.

Once again national security was used to drive an ideological public school reform agenda. Perhaps it was the sense of national inferiority to the Soviets that drove many to uncritically accept and endorse the report. Virtually every state board of education and local school board, whose members knew little about the history of American education, put their support behind the report or mentioned the report when they attempted to drive local reforms.

Of course the report's writers also referred to Sputnik and used it as the springboard for federal intervention into schooling. The report was loaded with antischool agendas, spurious studies, and cause-and-effect fallacies that would choke any speech teacher. A few sample quotes should give you the flavor of *A Nation at Risk.*

- "Our once unchallenged preeminence in commerce, industry, science, and technological innovation is being overtaken by competitors throughout the world" (p. 6). Now what does this have to do with public schools? That has more to do with monetary, labor, trade, and tax policy than with how students score on a standardized test (Cremin, 1989).
- " . . . the educational foundations of our society are presently being eroded by a rising tide of mediocrity that threatens our very future as a Nation and people" (p. 6). This assertion was plugged into the report with *virtually* no supporting evidence or detailed documentation.
- " . . . 23 million adults are functionally illiterate by the simplest tests of reading, writing, and comprehension" (p. 8). The writers never told us what tests they were referencing. To our knowledge, adults were not mandated to take any such tests in the 1980s or any other time before.

- "The average achievement of high school students on most standardized tests is lower than it was 26 years ago when Sputnik was
  launched" (p. 8). Interesting statement. At the time, 1983, there was
  only one test that could have been used to make this claim about
  high school students: the Iowa Test of Educational Development
  (ITED). Not every student in the country took that test. It is true
  that achievement on that test did decline during the late 1960s to
  the mid 1970s. Then achievement rose, unabated for 10 years, when
  in 1985, student achievement on the ITED was at an all-time high
  (Bracey, 2003).
- "Average tested achievement of students graduating college is also
  lower" (p. 9). No mention of what tests. There was not a mandated
  college exit exam.
- "The College Board's Scholastic Aptitude Tests (SAT) demonstrate
  a virtually unbroken decline from 1963 to 1980. Average verbal
  scores fell over 50 points and average mathematics scores dropped
  nearly 40 points" (pp. 8–9).

The last point about the SAT scores declining could be due to a confluence of several factors. There is no doubt that the aggregate scores declined, but why and so what? First, the statistical phenomenon known as
Simpson's Paradox could contribute to part of the decline. The general
idea behind Simpson's Paradox is that the results and conclusions from
an aggregate group data set are sometimes different than the results and
conclusions from the underlying subgroup data sets.

Remember there were more nontraditional (not college-bound) students taking the test at the time right before *Risk* was published than had
taken it historically. This was due in part to the push for educational
equality for traditionally underrepresented groups. More students who
had no interest in college and did not take college-level course work in
high school were encouraged to take the SAT to show that the opportunity to attend college was being offered to nontraditional college-type
students.

Also, the mid-1960s through the early 1970s was a time of great cultural upheaval in this country. To think that social forces did not influence
education outcomes is a bit naïve. One should also ask, so what if the
scores drop? What do they tell us anyway? The SAT was never designed
to measure education quality, and at best the SAT scores predict only
about 10 percent to 20 percent of a college student's first-year grade point
average (Korbin et al., 2008). We are not sure if national education policy
should be based on a dip in SAT scores. We provide more information on
this issue in the next section.

Keep in mind that the school reformers use a similar claim today of
stagnating test scores, but they do it often with the National Assessment
of Education Progress (NAEP). Sometimes referred to as the Nation's

Report Card, the NAEP is administered to a representative sample of public and private school students through the U.S. Department of Education. Subject-area tests are given on a rotating basis every two to four years.

The scale-score results from the NAEP seem particularly susceptible to misinterpretation due to Simpson's Paradox. For example, from 1975 to 2008 the NAEP reading scores for nine-year-olds improved only 10 scale-score points from 210 to 220. However, when one looks at the subgroup NAEP reading scores for that same age group from 1975 to 2008, it is easy to see the astounding growth made by all subgroups. (See table 2.1.) Black students made 23 scale-score points of progress from 181 to 204, more than double the aggregate progress.

Hispanic students made 24 scale-score points of progress from 183 to 207, more than double the aggregate progress. White students also outpaced the aggregate with 11 scale-score points of progress from 217 to 228. Simpson's Paradox comes into play because more lower-scoring students make up a greater proportion of the population (i.e., Blacks and Hispanics) compared to higher-scoring White students. Thus, the aggregate gain looks depressed, when in reality the minority subgroups' growth is more than double that of the Whites. This is a function of shifting demographics, poor economic policies, and a withering social safety net. Are our schools really failing our minority students, or is it something else?

A similar phenomenon occurs with NAEP mathematics scores. For example, the NAEP mathematics aggregate scale scores for students aged

Table 2.1. Subgroup Age 9 NAEP Reading Scale Scores

Year	White	Black	Hispanic
2008	228	204	207
2004	226	200	205
1999	221	186	193
1996	220	191	195
1994	218	185	186
1992	218	185	192
1990	217	182	189
1988	218	189	194
1984	218	186	187
1980	221	189	190
1975	217	181	183

Source: Public Domain

13 rose 17 points between 1978 and 2008 from 264 to 281. However, once again, the subgroup scores for Blacks, Hispanics, and Whites all outpaced the aggregate growth. But the scores for Blacks and Hispanics started out much lower compared to that of Whites.

The 1978 scale score for Blacks was 230, and it was 238 for Hispanics, whereas Whites started at 272, a difference of 42 and 34 points respectively. By 2008 scores for Whites rose to 290, a gain of 18 points, 262 for Blacks, and 268 for Hispanics. Blacks gained 32 points, almost double the gain made by Whites, and Hispanics gained 30 points. (See table 2.2.) The gap between Blacks and Whites closed to 28 points by 2008 compared to 42 points in 1978, a gain of 14 points. The gap between Hispanics and Whites closed to 22 points in 2008 compared to 34 points, a gain of 12 points.

Regardless that *A Nation at Risk* was an intellectually vapid and data-challenged piece of propaganda, many state education bureaucrats plunged headlong into reform movements, based on the advice of the presidential commission that wrote the report. *A Nation at Risk* recommended tougher course work requirements for high school graduation, higher admissions standards for universities, a longer school day and school years, merit pay for outstanding teachers, and more participation by citizens in the public schools.

As a blueprint, *Risk* offered nothing that had not been urged and discarded during the twentieth century. In fact Edson (1983) concluded that *A Nation at Risk* very closely resembles the 1893 report issued by the Committee of Ten. Membership on the Committee of Ten and the National Commission on Excellence in Education was dominated by non–public school personnel. The reports of both groups included recommendations

Table 2.2.   Subgroup Age 13 NAEP Mathematics Scale Scores

Year	White	Black	Hispanic
2008	290	262	268
2004	289	261	264
1999	283	251	259
1996	281	252	256
1994	281	252	256
1992	279	250	259
1990	276	249	255
1986	274	249	254
1982	274	240	252
1978	272	230	238

Source: Public Domain

that were worn out. Both groups recommended longer school terms, for example, and endorsed a brand of social Darwinism: the survival of the academically fittest.

Education reforms have been suggested for decades by individuals, foundations, associations, governmental agencies, university boards of regents, state boards of education, and local school boards. Too frequently, however, the suggested reforms were contradictory in nature, poorly implemented, not based on independently verified empirical evidence, and, eventually, abandoned. There are several reasons for the massive failure of the reform hamster wheel.

Many of the suggested reforms have been purely cosmetic; they have had no profound impact on instructional strategies, on the organization of schools, or on student learning. Simply put, most of the suggested reforms were *intrinsically inferior*, the products of armchair theorists who suggest simplistic solutions to complex educational and social problems, with no supporting research evidence.

More than 275 local and state education task forces were organized in the United States in the early and mid-1980s. The outcomes, according to Bill Chance (1988), included more requirements for graduation from high school in at least 43 states, higher college admissions standards in 17 states, statewide student assessment programs in 37 states, teacher competency tests in 29 states, and changes in teacher certification requirements in 28 states. Most school reform, Chance suggests, is slogan driven, political, and ephemeral.

NEVER ANY SIDE EFFECTS

Good researchers state the limitations of their studies. Unfortunately, writers of reform literature ignore major limitations, assumptions, and omissions. In fact we have found no contraindications listed from the vendors of the No Child Left Behind series of policies and practices, nor from those that champion the Common Core State Standards and national testing.

It is as if any idea that standardizes, centralizes, and mechanizes education for the majority and provides more opportunities for the wealthy minority has no downside. Yet, like so many reformers before them, the bulk of all national or state reformers failed to heed James Conant's advice that U.S. high schools should be improved at the local level, "school by school."

A CROWN CRUMBLES: THE SANDIA REPORT OBLITERATES *RISK*

Two definitions of fraud provided by the Merriam-Webster Online Dictionary are *deceit* and *trickery*. The unscientific and empirically absent claims made by the authors of *A Nation At Risk* seem at least deceitful, maybe even lies. The authors provided no empirical evidence to support their rhetoric, whereas empirical evidence existed to the contrary.

The publication of *Perspectives on Education in America* (Carson, Huelskamp & Woodall, 1993), known as the Sandia Report because it was conducted by the Sandia National Laboratory at the request of then secretary of energy Admiral James Watkins, demonstrated that *A Nation at Risk* was, in our opinion, a fraud. The study challenged the assertions made in *Risk* and did so on an empirical level, with data.

The report was actually completed in 1990 but was suppressed by then deputy secretary of the U.S. Department of Education under President George H. W. Bush, former Xerox CEO Dave Kearns. Kearns was reported to say at a meeting with the Sandia researchers that either the researchers should suppress the report and not release it or they would be suppressed (Miller, 1991). Suppression makes sense when one considers the conservative political climate of the time and the positive results of the report.

President George H. W. Bush was presiding over a tanking economy and recession. The Republican White House needed a scapegoat, and the public education system, once again, was there for the chiding. Bush needed to pin the recession on something other than faulty trickle-down economic policy. The fraud perpetrated in *A Nation at Risk* worked once before, and members of the administration saw a way to recycle the argument of a weak economy caused by a supposedly poor education system.

However, the Sandia Report painted a picture of a successful public education system. Some of the major findings of the report were:

- The high school graduation rate increased steadily since 1970 and the dropout rate had declined.
- Between 1960 and 1990 the percentage of the population aged 25 through 29 who completed high school rose over 30 percentage points to 7 out of every 8 persons in the age category.
- The dropout rates for Blacks and Whites declined steadily between 1968 and 1990, whereas the rate remained somewhat stable for Hispanics, due mostly to first-generation immigrants failing to complete high school.
- Approximately 83 percent of the class of 1982 completed high school on time (four years) and 91 percent earned a diploma or GED.
- Average SAT scores declined 5 percent between 1965 and 1990. The decline in SAT scores was attributed to changing demographics of the test takers to include more minorities and lower socioeconomic students, more students who were not college bound, and more students from lower high school class ranks.

In fact, when the demographic makeup of the test takers is held constant to that of the class of 1975, SAT scores rise unabated between 1975 and 1990: Simpson's Paradox at work. More students from the bottom half of their high school class took the SAT, whereas proportionately fewer students at the top 20 percent of their class took the test. Not exactly the crisis the Bush I administration was looking for.

The authors of the Sandia Report further noted that the number of bachelor's and master's degrees awarded increased 20 percent and 25 percent respectively between 1971 and 1987, and the Graduate Record Exam (GRE) math scores rose 32 points between 1973 and 1988, whereas the verbal scores remained stable. Furthermore the United States led the world in 1987 with the percentage of 22-year-olds obtaining a bachelor's degree in science and engineering.

The results from the Sandia Report demonstrated that the system was not at risk; in fact, it was performing quite well given the massive demographic, social, and political changes faced by the nation between 1963 and 1982. The Sandia Report exposed the factors listed in *A Nation at Risk* s indicators of risk as empirically lacking. We encourage readers of this book to examine *A Nation at Risk* and attempt to determine which data are referenced by the authors and where the data were found. It is difficult, but also amusing. The report can be found at www.ed.gov/pubs/NatAtRisk/risk.html. For a brief, easy-to-read, nonstatistical debunking of the report, see Bracey (1999) at www.america-tomorrow.com/bracey/EDDRA/EDDRA8.htm.

POINTS TO REMEMBER

Although widely discredited, *A Nation at Risk* continues to provide false legitimacy and mythology to those who covertly, under the banners of school choice, charter schools, or school vouchers, attempt to energize the movement toward a dual system of education.

A LOOK AHEAD

In the next chapter we present and dissect some of the most common school reform fallacies. Examples include the seemingly unending chorus from corporate privateers and wannabe business tycoons that education needs to be run more like a business. We discuss eight such fallacies in an attempt to demonstrate that most reform claims rest more on a bed of sand than of concrete.

REFERENCES

Berliner, D. C. & Biddle, B. J. (1995). *The Manufactured Crisis: Myths, Frauds and the Attack on America's Public Schools.* Reading, MA: Addison-Wesley.

Bon Jovi, J. & Sambora, R. (1995). These Days. On *These Days* [CD]. Nashville: Mercury Records.

Bracey, G. (1999). The propaganda of "A Nation at Risk." Retrieved from www.america-tomorrow.com/bracey/EDDRA/EDDRA8.htm.

Bracey, G. (2003). April Foolishness: The 20th Anniversary of *A Nation at Risk. Phi Delta Kappan* 84(8): 616–621.

Bushaw, W. J. & McNee, J. A. (September 2009). Americans Speak Out: Are Educators and Policy Makers Listening? *Phi Delta Kappan* 91(1): 9–29.

Carnegie Corporation. (1963, January). *Carnegie Corporation of New York Quarterly: Education and Politics.* 11(1). Author.

Carson, C. C., Huelskamp, R. M., & Woodall, T. D. (1993). Perspectives on Education in America. *The Journal of Educational Research* 86(5): 259–309.

Chance, W. (1988). *The Best of Educations.* Denver: Education Commission of the States.

Cremin, L. J. (1989). *Popular Education and Its Discontents.* New York: Harper and Row.

Duncan, A. (2009, October 16). Partners for Success: Secretary Arne Duncan's Remarks to the National Association of State Boards of Education Oct. 16, 2009. Retrieved from www.ed.gov/news/speeches/2009/10/10162009.html.

Edson, C. H. (1983). Risking the Nation. *Issues in Education* 1: 171–184.

Eisenhower, D. D. (1957, November 13). Text of address on "Our Future Security" delivered by the president in Oklahoma City. Subjects include military programs and satellite projects. Retrieved from www.presidency.ucsb.edu/ws/index.php?pid=10950&st=&st1=.

Gleason, E. S. (1957, October 10). National Security Council Discussion at the 339th Meeting of the National Security Council. NSC Series, Box 9, Eisenhower Papers, 1953–1961 (Ann Whitman File), Dwight D. Eisenhower Library, Abilene, Kansas. Retrieved from www.eisenhower.archives.gov/research/Digital_Documents/Sputnik/10-11-57.pdf.

Goodpaster, A. J. (1957a, October 9). Memorandum of conference with the President, October 8, 1957. The National Archives. ARC Identifier 186623. Retrieved from www.archives.gov/education/lessons/sputnik-memo/#documents.

Goodpaster, A. J. (1957ab, October 15). Memorandum of conference with the President on American science education and Sputnik DDE's Papers as President, DDE Diary Series, Box 27, October '57 Staff Notes (2). Retrieved from www.eisenhower.archives.gov/research/Digital_Documents/Sputnik/10-16-57.pdf.

Klein, N. (2008). *Shock Doctrine: The Rise of Disaster Capitalism.* London: Picador.

Korbin, J. L., Patterson, B. F., Shaw, E. J., Mattern, K. D. & Barbuti, S. M. (2008). V*alidity of the SAT for Predicting First-Year College Grade Point Average.* New York: The College Board.

Lakoff, G. (2004). *Don't Think of an Elephant.* White River Junction, VT: Chelsea Green Publishing.

Mathews, D. & N. McAfee. (2003). *Making Choices Together: The Power of Public Deliberation.* Dayton, OH: Kettering Foundation.

Miller, J. (9 October, 1991). Report Questioning "Crisis" in Education Triggers an Uproar. *Education Week.* Retrieved from: www.edweek.org/ew/articles/1991/10/09/06crisis.h11.html.

Murray, T. S. (1999). "International Adult Literacy Household Survey Methods." In *Literacy: An International Handbook,* D. A. Wagner, R. L. Venezky and B. V. Street (Eds.). Boulder, CO: Westview Press, pp. 217–223.

National Commission on Excellence in Education. (1983). *A Nation at Risk.* Washington, DC: U.S. Department of Education.

National Defense Education Act. *U.S. Statutes at Large: 85th Congress, 2nd Session, 1958,* page 1580.

Obama, B. H. (2009, April 27). Remarks by the President at the National Academy of Science Annual Meeting. Retrieved from www.whitehouse.gov/the_press_office/Remarks-by-the-President-at-the-National-Academy-of-Sciences-Annual-Meeting/.

Paige, R. (2003, February 5). The Secretary's Mathematics and Science Initiative. Retrieved from www.ed.gov/rschstat/research/progs/mathscience/describe.html.

Rich, A. (2005). War of Ideas: Why Mainstream and Liberal Foundations and the Think Tanks They Support Are Losing the War of Ideas in American Politics. *Stanford Social Innovation Review* Spring: 18–25.

Riley, R. (1995, March 13). U.S. Secretary of Education before the Subcommittee on Human Resources and Intergovernmental Affairs of the House Committee on Government Reform and Oversight. Retrieved from www.ed.gov/Speeches/03-1995/shays.html.

Time. (1982, April 26). A boost for private schools: Reagan offers tax credits. Retrieved from www.cnn.com/ALLPOLITICS/1997/04/28/back.time/.

United States Census Bureau. (2009). Educational attainment in the United States. Population characteristics. Author. Retrieved from: www.census.gov/hhes/socdemo/education.

THREE

A Catalogue of Reform Fallacies

In this chapter we present eight self-evident fallacies associated with the modern reform movement, the movement born from Sputnik and determined to create a dual system of education driven by the fracturing, marketizing, and privatization of public schools and the co-opting of public funds.

Each of the fallacies is what those who live in the western United States call "a box canyon," or a three-sided ravine used to trap the minds of the complacent. Ultimately, we predict these fallacies will create an anti-reform backlash if educators and the general public apply a skeptical eye to the current reform agenda.

FALLACY 1. GOVERNMENT COERCION WILL ACCELERATE STUDENT ACHIEVEMENT

Student achievement has been monitored over most of the past 100 years by a battery of tests. In general, the results show an upward trend in student achievement. As pointed out in chapter 2, the subgroup scores for at least the mathematics, science, and language arts portions of the NAEP demonstrated remarkable growth for more than 30 years. Admittedly, we have not reviewed the scores for the other NAEP tests because the reform movements since Sputnik have only really focused on math, language arts, and science.

It must be recognized that more students are taking the ACT and SAT examinations than ever. Included in the additional takers are more students from lower socioeconomic strata of all races. Further, as the Sandia Report (Carson, Huelskamp & Woodall, 1993) illustrated, more students in the bottom half of classes are taking the SAT than in years past. Poverty has a negative impact on standardized test results. So, although the national test indicators have risen very slowly, the SAT shows that the students in all subgroups, especially non-Whites, are achieving at rather modestly higher levels.

A unique and fairer way to judge the performance of schools would be to compare test takers of the past and present who were alike in class ranking. This is what researchers at the Sandia Laboratories did (Carson et al., 1993). They selected a group of students from the 1990 SAT test takers who matched in gender and class ranking those students who took the test in 1975.

When the researchers compared the two groups' average scores, the 1990 group outscored the 1975 group by 30 points, on a scale of 800. These results are consistent with the NAEP trends we presented earlier. Furthermore, the Sandia Report found that NAEP scores of nine-, thirteen-, and seventeen-year-olds made steady gains in reading and math from 1971 to 1988. Other studies show that in areas such as social studies, students know about as much as previous groups.

The basic premise of modern-day state and national educational reform is that achievement is at an all-time low and educators and students must be coerced to improve it. Education reform policies based on coercion lack theoretical and empirical foundations and are not scientifically demonstrated. They are utterly anti-intellectual. Anti-intellectualism is an interesting approach for an endeavor based in part on intellectual development.

Advocates of coercion-based policies, such as common curriculum standards monitored by high-stakes standardized exams, generally harvest policy frameworks from rational choice theory and behaviorist theories of cognitive development. The frameworks are operationalized via state education policies that use positive reinforcement and negative reinforcement, also known as carrots and sticks. Bryk and Hermanson (1993) termed this an instrumental use model.

The theory is that a policy body develops a set of expected education outcome measures (e.g., state standards), monitors the relationship between the measures and school processes, usually through high-stakes testing, and then implements rewards or sanctions to change behavior through external force to maximize performance. The measures rest upon arbitrary achievement proficiency levels and external control.

For example, advocates of high school exit exam policies postulate that high-stakes exit exams cause students and teachers to work harder and achieve more because the tests create teaching and learning targets that have perceived meanings to both groups. In other words, they will make a "rational choice" to work harder to prepare for the exams.

Of course, there is an underlying assumption in the theoretical framework that teachers and students do not work hard, and therefore need external motivators to improve. Another example includes the threats from SEAs (State Education Agencies) to withhold funding for poor performance on high-stakes tests to compel school personnel to work harder because they do not want to lose funding. A similar version is the use of public castigation via the press and ratings and/or rankings of districts by SEA personnel to spur educators to work harder to achieve outcomes.

One major weakness of policies harvested from behaviorist and rational choice theories is that they do not have a demonstrated record of success. That is because behaviorism rests upon the idea of control. Stimulus-response psychology is at the heart of behaviorism "science for controlling others" (Bredo, 2002, 25). We doubt seriously that policies created from theories and science based on controlling others have a part in a free, participative democracy.

Furthermore, we see a disconnect between a public education system charged with the development of innovative thinking, creative thinking, strategizing, and problem solving and a public education system being directed and managed through policies based on control and predictable output. The irony is staggering.

Conversely, opponents of coercive policies derive theoretical guidance from an enlightenment model based on self-determination theory (Laitsch, 2006). Creators of an assessment system based on an enlightenment model seek to foster greater discussion, study, and reflection of education practices based on the indicators of the assessment system. Standardized tests still play a part, but their uses and interpretations are different compared to those within an instrumental use model.

Collective Punishment

An interesting characteristic about the current education policies at the state and national levels, and the one that is foreshadowed in the Common Core State Standards movement to nationalize curriculum standards and testing and the Race to the Top (RTTT) program, is that they mirror closely something known as collective punishment. Collective punishment is a policy of punishing a large group for the actions of a small group.

It should be known that the Soviets utilized collective punishment on a regular basis to control populations. The British used the strategy during the years leading up to the American Revolution through the implementation of the Intolerable Acts. There are countless other examples throughout history of authoritarian nations using collective punishment to force their political wills on the population.

An education system that models policies based in part on collective punishment seems unconstitutional because such policies appear to violate due process rights. It is certainly not a good way to model democratic behavior to future bearers of democratic ideals. Are not those who are punished supposed to receive a due process hearing? As taxpayers, we are requesting ours.

In essence, the carrots and sticks used in instrumental use policies have little effect, and might have negative effects, if the people believe that they are in a no-win situation. Coercion, intimidation, collective punishment, and policies based on broken theories and anti-intellectualism are unnecessary, not productive, and border on institutional abuse.

The Role of Mandated High-Stakes Standardized Testing

"Testing" now plays the key role in educational reform to show increased student achievement. Batteries of tests tend to be state-designed. Key states, such as Texas, California, Florida, Massachusetts, Michigan, Arizona, Washington, and Oregon, created assessments that allegedly measure student competence in a variety of subject areas. However, the testing movement made a huge evolutionary leap forward when almost all state education agencies approved the use of two standardized tests to measure the CCSS.

In essence, these education bureaucrats nationalized high-stakes standardized testing; but at what cost and based on what evidence? There is much evidence that the nation's previous large-scale testing experiment did not help students achieve liberty and justice.

Evidence suggests that some of the learning objectives embedded in the CCSS will be out of the mastery range of large percentages of children in each grade level. Thus, one could expect that at least some of the questions on the national standardized tests will also be out of the cognitive mastery range of some students. Even a cursory understanding of Piaget's developmental levels compared to a grade level breakdown of the CCSS demonstrates that some of the discrete learning objectives embedded in the larger macro-standards, and some of the macro-standards themselves, will be out of reach of mastery.

Yet the CCSS are all mastery mandated. The results from Porter et al. (2011) demonstrated that the cognitive load of the CCSS increased when compared to existing state standards at several grade levels in mathematics and English language arts. If portions of the CCSS are outside of the development levels of the students subjected to those standards, will the questions used on the national tests be any better? Can we not do better in this country than relying on Soviet-style coercion and fear?

FALLACY 2. BIG BUSINESS VALUES WILL IMPROVE PUBLIC EDUCATION

Close to the center of a large education box canyon is the not-so-quietly-kept assumption that the values of big business should be incorporated into the culture of the schools. Nationally "Achieve, Inc." is a business advocacy group aimed at "reforming" the nation's schools. This is a corporate group, and in 2001 it was cochaired by Louis V. Gerstner, Jr., chairman and CEO, IBM Corporation. Achieve, Inc., also has six state governors along with six corporate CEOs on its board of directors (*Achieve Policy Brief, #1, 2000*). We find the "Inc." portion of the name intriguing. You bet this is a dramatic focus on the business model. And there is not one schoolteacher in any of their employ or on that national board.

Business Core Values

What are the core values of American big business? Inarguably, the hallmark of American business is maximizing shareholder value, known as profits, and competition. The value of competition appears explicitly in every business-oriented educational "partnership" or "educational roundtable." Competition is exemplified by big business support of competitive testing for students and states as well. It shows up as support for "educational vouchers" or for "charter schools."

The following list seems to be made up of very apparent business values: (a) Competition, takeover, and monopoly; (b) The "bottom line" as all important regardless of the means; (c) Communities and workers are expendable, management is not; (d) Loyalty is not a mutual trait; (e) Workers obey management without questioning: dissent is not permitted; (f) Products are sought at the cheapest price; and (g) The importance of an individual is related to his or her net dollar worth.

Granted, these may show some writer bias, but remember that our biases lead us to prefer policies and practices based on evidence and that help children become participating members of society and help them to question the status quo in order to pursue liberty and justice for all. We prefer policies and practices that facilitate all children attaining liberty and justice, not just those whose parents can afford to purchase those things.

Read any issue of the *Wall Street Journal* or *Forbes* magazine and you will have to agree with the overall basic premise of business: Business leaders care about business, and business is about profit. Noam Chomsky (2011) eloquently explained that business leaders in most cases will put profit above people. In fact, in most publicly traded companies, it is the primary job of the CEO to maximize shareholder value (higher profits = higher share price). This is not a secret.

In her critical analysis of business values as espoused by the National Center on Education and the Economy, Diana M. Fessler (1996) vividly and with an abundance of evidence described how business interests are attempting to modify all American schools to provide cheap labor, not a liberal education. The U.S. economy depends on a steady source of cheap labor. In fact, evidence suggests that the number of illegal immigrants that flow in and out of the country correlates strongly to the U.S. labor market needs (Passel, 2006).

Remember that since the Reagan administration in the 1980s, both political parties have controlled the Congress and the presidency at least one time for a span of at least two years, yet the Congress and president never passed the meaningful immigration "reform" about which they spoke on the campaign trails: ending illegal immigration. Both parties know that if they ended illegal immigration and either deported the illegal workers from the country or gave them a path to citizenship, labor costs would rise, followed by prices of goods.

One way or another, unregulated capitalism requires a cheap source of labor, whether legislators create that source by turning a blind eye to illegal immigration or they create it through high school dropouts, or a combination of both. Whatever the ways, business values will continue to be geared toward profit maximization and not toward liberty and justice for all.

Broken Values

We boldly suggest that business values are not appropriate to drive American education. True, we all want the most efficient use of the tax-payer dollar in the public schools. But that is not an educational core value. Certainly, parents want their children to receive that elusive "best of educations." But business-like competitive practices are unlikely to provide it. Democracy is not efficient and thus, a democratic education is not efficient. In fact, it is the inefficiency in the system that perhaps produces some its greatest qualities among American students: creativity and innovation.

Yong Zhao (2012) masterfully explains how the U.S. system, although historically decentralized and inefficient, has created one of the most dynamic, innovative, and entrepreneurial workforces on the planet, while more centralized and standardized systems like China, Singapore, and South Korea strive to catch up.

Similar arguments are dramatically illustrated in *The Manufactured Crisis: Myth, Fraud, and the Attack on America's Public Schools* (Berliner and Biddle, 1995). The cult of efficiency, as earlier described by Raymond E. Callahan (1962), is being forced upon the public schools without organized objection by teachers, students, or administrators.

Our conclusion is that big business interests are now in the process of "conditioning" the American public (recall Pavlov's dog) so that the European dual system of education might ultimately replace the current state and local control system. In parts of Europe and most other countries, children, as we have already noted, are tested and then grouped into two irrevocable tracks—university bound or trade and industry bound. For one reason or another, Americans are not questioning that such a system has not provided other nations with acclaimed industrial leadership or leadership in most any academic realm.

Much of the above discussion implies that business leaders are attempting to *privatize* public education. John E. Chubb and Terry M. Moe (1990) are apologists for school vouchers. They argue that private school vouchers, paid by taxpayers, are needed because the public schools are incapable of reforming themselves due to bureaucratic and political restraints. They then praise private schools as exhibiting superior academic performance.

As Alex Molnar (1999) observed, the research on the topic has no clear evidence showing private schools to be better than public schools. We'd add, with a small enough sample, you can prove anything. Lubienski and Lubienski (2006) conducted a thorough review of the data and found that the claim that private school students do better academically than public school students was in fact flawed.

Lubienski found that the achievement gains of students are similar when comparing "like" students' results on the mathematics portion of the National Assessment of Education Progress (NAEP), and the public schools achieve those gains cheaper than private schools.

If you really must impose a business model on the public schools, the model should be that of a regulated utility. The schools are a giant public utility, established to promote the public welfare. We all acknowledge that there are bad schools, poor teachers, inept administrators, and parsimonious legislators.

Yet a public utility delivers its services to all that sign up—or in the case of the traditional public schools, those who show up at the schoolhouse door no matter what social baggage they bring. Achieve, Inc., and its clones ignore that feature. And they totally ignore Enron, Tyco, Global Crossing, J. P. Morgan Chase, Barclays Bank, World COM, Arthur Andersen, Imclone, Piper Jaffray, Goldman Sachs, Bear Stearns, and all those other manipulative corporations and investment banking houses, their senior analysts, and traders on the stock exchanges. The business path to reform is a very muddy detour at best. Its players may praise ethics, but practicing them seems to be a problem.

FALLACY 3. INTUITIVELY DERIVED STANDARDS CAN REPLACE EMPIRICALLY DERIVED EDUCATIONAL SOLUTIONS

An analysis of the many sets of reform standards that have emerged in the United States reveal none that are based on empirical studies. The standards are constructed via a committee of representative teachers, researchers, university scholars, or interested citizens. In this sense, the standards are simply dogmatic pronouncements of what children in elementary, middle, and secondary schools "should" master.

The standards movement is a classic example of authoritarianism. In no case has there been field-testing of any of the standards to determine their developmental appropriateness. An example of how absurd the setting of standards can be is in the state of Washington.

The state superintendent proudly announced, in print and word, the following for fourth-graders: in determining the level, the committee was guided by what they believed a "well-taught, hard-working student" should be able to do in the spring of the fourth grade. This was claimed to be "thorough expert judgment." Yes, uh-huh. Wouldn't you enjoy seeing what amateurs would come up with? Sadly, this may well be the norm for standard-setters.

There is one model of standardization that is empirically tested, and that is the Tennessee model showing that class size standardizing to 13 to 17 students improves student achievement. Let us briefly discuss the American Educational Research Association's special publication "Class Size: Issues and New Findings" in *Educational Evaluation and Policy Analysis*, Volume 21, Number 2, Summer 1999. America's leading education research association wanted to provide a "bully pulpit" to announce the validated research studies on small class size (Finn & Achilles, 1999). What makes the issue interesting is that critics of the study were also provided a platform. In total, the evidence supporting the impact on student achievement appears to be irrefutable. The argument focuses on "Is the amount of effect that class size has on student achievement worth the price tag?"

In the race to create "world-class" standards, the Tennessee STAR study is completely ignored as a *competing model*. Isn't this ironic? The business leaders of America, who advocate standards totally, disregard a competing model. Note: competing model—is this not what the business sector titans want? The answer is a resounding NO! Empirical studies muddy authoritarian praise for standards. The small-class-size path does lead to meaningful reform, while standards, per se, tend to get us all lost in the dark educational reform forest.

FALLACY 4. STANDARDS ARE TECHNICAL SPECIFICATIONS BEING CONFUSED WITH, BUT APPLIED TO, HUMAN LEARNING CAPABILITIES

An observation of the many sets of standards shows misapplication of technical specifications to human nature. Each published standard resembles a product specification. For example, most begin with a statement that the student will ----- (just fill in the blank). Replace the student with a battery and the specifications are that the battery will light a three-watt bulb for two hours.

Such technically oriented pronouncements of student achievement lack mention of the conditions under which the learning is to take place and completely ignore the needed educational prerequisites and materials required to learn. This dimension of the standards movement is plainly *dehumanizing the educational process*. Students are now simply objects to be manipulated.

We suggest reading Martin Buber (1971) in which he vividly illustrates how your actions toward fellow human beings are shown in how you perceive them. If you view children, adolescents, or early adults only as objects rather than as humans to be nurtured, then schooling takes on a mechanistic dimension. Jonathan Kozol (2005) shockingly illustrates how standards and high-stakes tests become more important than the cultivation of a child's potential.

An unintentional result of not realizing Fallacy 4 is that schools are now, more than ever, considered assembly lines of knowledge. Students are products. Such industrial metaphors are completely inappropriate for delicate human endeavors. Yet, these same technical specifications are praised as *the* means for reaching those dubious world-class standards.

Children, we must caution, are not machines with specified tolerance values, voltage regulators, or assembled packages. Editorial writers and industrialists who heap praise and advocate adoption of standards show a bias to industrial values. *Pervasive caring* is a quality found in the best schools in this country. Caring, empathy, and love are not listed in any educational or business standard, but they are found in the best of schools.

The notions of caring, empathy, and love imply that the school is a safe haven. A place you can visit, make friends, be accepted even if you're poor, smell funny, have an unpronounceable name, walk slower than the rest of the kids, or have pigmented skin. Caring, empathy, and love mean that even if you arrive with heavy social baggage, someone in the school will lend a hand—the janitor, a secretary, the principal, your peers, your teachers. These three notions profoundly affect how children are respected and how they enjoy the challenge to learn. In some cases the school is the only setting where students feel they are valued, loved, and cared about.

FALLACY 5. HIGH-STAKES, STATE-MANDATED TESTING AND ASSESSMENT PROGRAMS WILL INCREASE STUDENT LEARNING

The bulk of published studies show that high-stakes testing has not had a significant effect on student achievement. However, two exemplars from the Consortium for Policy Research in Education at the University of Pennsylvania do illustrate the problem of generalizing. Reviewing data nationally and internationally, John B. Bishop (1998) concluded that cur-

riculum-based external exit examinations did increase student achievement. In 2001, Martin Carnoy, Susanna Loeb, and Tiffany L. Smith reported that in Texas there was a rising pass rate on the Texas Assessment
of Academic Skills (TAAS) test, but there appears to be a confounding
correlation to high school minority student graduate rates.

Walt Haney (2000) reported that using the TAAS and comparing
scores with the SAT, academic learning by secondary school students had
not improved. In mathematics, they showed a decline, although there
have been "dramatic" gains in the TAAS. His concluding sentence tells
all. "The Texas 'miracle' is more hat than cattle."

Speaking of the Lone Star State, it must be reported that the dropout
rate for minority children, especially Blacks and Hispanics, rose precipi-
tously after Bush II assumed the governorship and throughout the NCLB
era. Walt Haney (August 19, 2000) found that "only 50% of minority
students in Texas have been progressing from grade 9 to high school
graduation since the initiation of the TAAS testing program."

Writing in the *New York Times*, August 13, 2003, Michael Winerip
reported how a Houston high school falsified its dropout data. No dropouts were reported from Westside High School, where actually 3,000
should have been counted as dropouts—mostly poor and minority. We
discuss high-stakes testing in a later chapter and provide more empirical
evidence about the lack of efficacy. Most studies show no gains, or gains
at a cost to other areas like SAT scores or high school graduation rates
that cause us to question the use of high-stakes testing. Are the costs
worth the possible small gains?

FALLACY 6. ALL HIGH SCHOOL STUDENTS WILL BENEFIT FROM REQUIRED ENROLLMENT IN COLLEGE PREPARATORY PROGRAMS

Recall that James B. Conant helped save the comprehensive American
high school. That institution provides the following options: (1) college
preparatory, (2) vocational, and (3) general education. But wait; guess
who provides unmitigated evidence to support Fallacy 6? Yep, none other than Marc S. Tucker! Writing with Judy C. Codding (1998), this dynamic duo suggested redefining the comprehensive high school into two
categories: "academics and applied academics" (p. 192).

Their model is the Danish national school system, and the ultimate
adoption of this model would provide an educational caste system in the
United States! Only 12 short years later that model was well on its way to
becoming a reality with the imposition of the CCSS enforced with a national high-stakes standardized test. We predict the test scores from the
national exams will be used to eventually sort students into high school

paths, thereby creating the dual system within the unitary system: a "school within a school" model if you will.

FALLACY 7. STUDENTS AND PARENTS ARE UNCONCERNED ABOUT THE PSYCHOLOGICAL ABUSES CAUSED BY "ONE-SIZE-FITS-ALL-STANDARDS" AND TESTING

The unintended consequences of the state and national standards movement have been rather well documented and for a long time. For example, in most states, if a student throws up on the state-mandated high-stakes standardized test, the school personnel are instructed to place all the contents into a sealed plastic bag and return it to the superintendent of public instruction. No directions are given on what to do with the child. Oh, and if your kid is in the hospital, well, a monitor will administer the state test and nurses will be observed for any cheating. Yes, sir, the state education bureaucrats created a system of world-class accountability.

To be more empirical and a bit more objective, Audrey L. Amrein and David C. Berliner (2002) illustrate the psychological abuses of high-stakes testing. Collecting data from 18 states with high-stakes tests, they noted that in 16 of 18 states high school dropout rates increased, graduation rates declined, and it appeared that students who score poorly on tests are actually being forced out.

Let us note that in the state of Minnesota in 2000, the scoring company NCS Pearson made thousands of errors on the state's high-stakes test, thus prohibiting hundreds of seniors from graduating. The courts have held for the students—psychological duress—and awarded approximately $12 million in damages to these individuals and their parents, attorney's fees, and court costs.

Norman Draper of the *Star Tribune* of Minneapolis reported on October 5, 2002, that NCS Pearson was sued in a class action suit by 7,900 of the 8,000 students on whom testing errors were made. The exact settlements ranged from $362.50 to $16,000, depending on selected criteria. Students denied graduation were each awarded $16,000. These students had their state basic-skills tests incorrectly graded by the company (see Court Order No. 00-11010).

Testing companies have made errors on New York City's high-stakes tests, resulting in reassignment of over 10,000 children to a special summer school, when in fact they should have been on vacation. Additionally Harcourt Educational Measurement Company admitted making errors on the Texas Assessment of Knowledge and Skills (TAKS) test. The math section had one mistake. In Texas, children will be detained in grade if they fail.

In Nevada, the same company used the wrong scoring table, causing third-and fifth-graders in 220 elementary schools to receive wrong tests. In Clark County (Las Vegas), 21,000 third- and fifth-grade students had incorrectly reported scores, noted Cy Ryan (2003) of the *Las Vegas Sun*. Oh, in 2002, Harcourt was fined $425,000 because they had informed 736 high school sophomores and juniors in Las Vegas that they had failed the proficiency test. Doesn't that news make you sleep better tonight?

It must be noted that 27,000 SAT tests taken in October 2005 had scoring errors. The errors could account for almost 20 percent of individuals' total exam score (Romano, 2006). A series of class action lawsuits have followed this little "technical glitch." For sure there are parental and student concerns about test abuses, but they are muffled by the sound of cash registers.

FALLACY 8. CENTRALIZATION OF EDUCATIONAL DECISION MAKING BENEFITS OUR NATION

If there is one truism, it is that the No Child Left Behind Act of 2001 was a clear and bold attempt to centralize America's three centuries of decentralized schools. Let us quote extensively from Richard F. Elmore (2002), who is writing for the very conservative Hoover Institution—hardly a gang of knee-jerk softies.

> The federal government is requiring annual testing at every grade level, and requiring states to disaggregate their test scores by racial and socioeconomic backgrounds—a system currently operating in only a handful of states and one that is fraught with technical difficulties. The federal government is mandating a single definition of adequate yearly progress, the amount by which schools must increase their test scores in order to avoid some sort of sanction—an issue that in the past has been decided jointly by states and the federal government. And the federal government has set a single target date by which all students must exceed a state-defined proficiency level—an issue that in the past has been left almost entirely to states and localities.
>
> Thus, the federal government is now accelerating the worst trend of the current accountability movement: that performance-based accountability has come to mean testing, and testing alone. It doesn't have to. In fact, in the early stages of the current accountability movement, reformers had an expansive view of performance that included, in addition to tests, portfolios of students' work, teachers' evaluations of their students, student-initiated projects, and formal exhibitions of students' work. The comparative appeal of standardized tests is easy to see: they are relatively inexpensive to administer; can be mandated relatively easily; can be rapidly implemented; and deliver clear, visible results. However, relying only on standardized tests simply dodges the complicated questions of what tests actually measure and of how

schools and students react when tests are the sole yardstick of performance. (pp. 1–2)

The NCLB Act stated that the federal government controls the nation's public schools. And considering that the federal government contributes about only 7 percent of the funding, this is classic "tail wagging the dog."

POINTS TO REMEMBER

Most of what is marketed to the general public regarding the principles of school reform seems to weaken under examination. The more we dig, the more we come to the conclusion that the late Soviet Union is the blueprint for current U.S. education reform. We can't help but come back to this comparison. In 1928, Marshal Joseph Stalin announced the first of what would be 13 five-year plans. The thirteenth plan was dumped when the "Evil Empire" dissolved in the 1990s.

Every Soviet five-year plan ended in a failure. We predict the same failure with America's first ever, Stalinist-inspired education plan. We rest our case. We have another reform path leading to nowhere. Now, let us examine in chapter 4 the No Child Left Behind Act itself. You can make your own decisions as to where that path leads.

A LOOK AHEAD

We provide a closer look at the No Child Left Behind Act and raise some questions about the underlying support for many of its provisions. We also question its efficacy in terms of strengthening the unitary, democratic system of education.

REFERENCES

Achieve, Inc. (2000). *Achieve Policy Brief* 1(1): 1–8.

Achilles, C. M., Nye, B. A., Zaharias, J. B. & Fulton, B. D. (1993). The Lasting Benefits Study (LBS) in grades 4 and 5 (1990–1991): A legacy from Tennessee's four-year (K–3) class-size study (1985–1989), Project STAR. Paper presented at the North Carolina Association for Research in Education. Greensboro, North Carolina, January 14, 1993.

American Educational Research Association. (Summer 1999). Class Size: Issues and New Findings. In *Educational Evaluation and Policy Analysis* 21(2).

Amrein, A. L. & Berliner, D. C. (2002, March 28). High-Stakes Testing, Uncertainty and Student Learning. *Educational Policy Analysis Archives* 10(18): 1–56. Retrieved April 1, 2002 from epasa.asu.edu/epaa/v10n18.

Berliner, D. C. & Biddle, B. J. (1995). *The Manufactured Crisis: Myths, Frauds and the Attack on America's Public Schools*. Reading, MA: Addison-Wesley.

Bishop, J. (1998). *Do Curriculum-Based External Exit Exam Systems Enhance Student Achievement?* Consortium for Policy Research in Education, University of Pennsylvania, CRPE, RR-40.

Bracey, G. W. (2003, February). NCLB—A Plan for the Destruction of Public Education: Just Say 'NO'! *No Childleft.com.* Vol. 1, No. 2. Accessed from nochildleft.com/2003/feb03no.html.

Bredo, E. (2002). The Darwinian Center to the Vision of William James. In Garrison, J., Poedeschi, P. & Bredo, E. (Eds.), *William James and Education.* New York: Teachers College Press.

Bryk, A. & Hermanson, K. (1993). Educational Indicator Systems: Observations on Their Structure, Interpretation and Use. In: L. Darling-Hammond, Ed., *Review of Research in Education* 19, American Educational Research Association, Washington, DC (1993): 451–484.

Buber, M. (1971). *I-Thou.* New York: Free Press.

Callahan, R. E. (1962). *Education and the Cult of Efficiency: A Study of the Social Forces That Have Shaped the Administration of Public Schools.* Chicago: University of Chicago Press.

Carnoy, M., Loeb, S. & Smith, T. L. (2001, November). *Do Higher State Test Scores in Texas Make for Better High School Outcomes?* Consortium for Policy Research in Education, University of Pennsylvania, CPRE, RR-047.

Carson, C. C., Huelskamp, R. M. & Woodall, T. D. (1993, May/June). Perspectives on Education in America: An Annotated Briefing. *Journal of Educational Research* 86(5): 259–310. This reports the Sandia National Laboratories (1993) *Perspectives on Education in America* [known as the Sandia Report]. Albuquerque, NM.

Chomsky, N. (2011). *Profit over People: Neoliberalism and Global Order.* New York, NY: Seven Stories Press.

Chubb, J. E. & Moe, T. M. (1990). *Politics, Markets and America's Schools.* Washington, DC: The Brookings Institution.

Court Order No. 00-11010. (2003, January 24). Order Granting Plaintiffs' Motion for Final Approval of Class Action Settlement and for Final Judgment. Fourth Judicial District Court, State of Minnesota, Hennepin County. Allen Oliskey, Judge.

Elmore, R. F. (2002, Spring). Unwarranted Intrusion. *Education Next.* The Hoover Institution. Retrieved on May 5, 2003: www.educationtext.org/20021/30.html.

Fessler, D. M. (1996, December 10). *A Report on the Work toward National Standards, Assessments and Certificates.* New Carlisle, OH. See www.fessler.com.

Finn, J. D. & Achilles, C. M. (1999). *Tennessee's Class Size Study: Findings, Implications, Misconceptions. Educational Evaluation and Policy Analysis.* Special Issue—Class Size: Issues and New Findings 21(2): 97–109. Washington, DC: American Educational Research Association.

Haney, W. (2000, August 19). The Myth of the Texas Miracle in Education. *Education Policy Analysis Archives* 8(41). Retrieved at epaa.asu.edu/epaa/v8n41.

Highlights from the Third International Mathematics and Science Study —Repeat (TIMSS-4). (2001). Washington, DC: National Center for Education Statistics, NCES 2001-027.

Houston's School Dropout Debacle. (2003, July 21). *The New York Times* editorial.

Indicators of Science and Mathematics Education 1995. (1996). Arlington, VA: National Science Foundation, NSF 96–52.

Kozol, J. (2005). *The Shame of the Nation: The Restoration of Apartheid Schooling in America.* New York: Crown Publishers, a Division of Random House.

Laitsch, D. (2006) Assessment, high stakes, and alternative visions: Appropriate use of the right tools to leverage improvement. Retrieved from epsl.asu.edu/epru/documents/EPSL-0611-222-EPRU.pdf .

Lubienski, C. & Lubienski, S. (2006). Charter, private, and public school academic achievement: New evidence from NAEP mathematics data. National Center for the Study of Privatization in Education. Teachers College, Columbia University. Retrived from epicpolicy.org/files/EPRU-0601-137-OWI[1].pdf.

Molnar, A. (1999, October). *Educational Vouchers: A Review of the Research*. Milwaukee, WI: Center for Education Research, Analysis and Innovation, University of Wisconsin–Milwaukee.

Nairn, A. (Ed.). (1980). *The Reign of ETS: The Corporation That Makes Up Minds*. Washington, DC: Ralph Nader Report.

National Commission on Excellence in Education. (1983). *A Nation at Risk: The Imperative for Educational Reform*. Washington, DC: Author.

No Child Left Behind (NCLB) Act of 2001, Pub. L. No. 107-110, § 115, Stat. 1425 (2002).

Passel, J. (2006). Size and Characteristics of the Unauthorized Migrant Population in the U.S. Pew Research Center. Retrieved from: www.pewhispanic.org/2006/03/07/size-and-characteristics-of-the-unauthorized-migrant-population-in-the-us/.

Porter, A., McMaken, J., Hwang, J. & Yang, R. (2011). Common Core Standards: The New U.S. Intended Curriculum. *Educational Researcher* 40: 103–116.

Romano, L. (2006, March 24). College Board Acknowledges More SAT Scoring Errors. *Washington Post*, All.

Ryan, C. (2003, August 22). School Testing Company Flunks Again. *Las Vegas Sun*, Nevada.

Tucker, M. S. & Codding, J. B. (1998). *Standards for Our Schools: How to Set Them, Measure Them and Reach Them*. San Francisco, CA: Jossey-Bass.

Winerip, M. (2003, August 13). The 'Zero Dropout Miracle.' Alas! Alack! A Texas Tall Tale. *New York Times*.

Zhao, Y. (2012). *World Class Learners: Educating Creative and Entrepreneurial Students*. Thousand Oaks, CA: Corwin Press.

FOUR

The No Child Left Behind Act

A critical review of the No Child Left Behind Act of 2001 (No Child Left Behind [NCLB PL 107-110], 2002) provides an opportunity to see the operationalization, at the national level, of overt education policy designed to create the dual system, a two-tiered education system, a reality. We now have the benefit of hindsight, and an understanding of the empirical evidence.

We are not trying to sensationalize the reach of the NCLB Act. It actually fits quite logically into the sequence of the modern reform movements toward a dual system of education given the rhetoric, reports, and legislation enacted before 2001. Based upon the prior empirical analyses of the influence of the Act on the public school system that have taken place since the enactment of the law, we can arrive at no other conclusion than that NCLB was meant to cripple the system. It was meant to once again create the education crisis that never existed, but was necessary to usher in a speedy descent to the dual system.

Assessment-driven education policies have been in place in all 50 states in the United States since the 2003–2004 school year. Although NCLB and CCSS accountability are two examples of assessment-driven legislation, the modern-day groundwork for recent federal education-reform initiatives was laid in 1978 with the release of the report *Improving Educational Achievement* (Committee on Testing and Basic Skills, 1978). That report seemed to be the foundation for the NCLB Act.

The authors of the 1978 report called for changes in schooling and recommended a return to "Basic Skills" and increased achievement-test scores as a goal of government, greater teacher quality, and test-score-driven accountability of teachers and administrators as ways to "improve" education. Several statements seem prophetic now. "American education should be paying much more attention to doing a thorough job in the fundamentals of reading, writing, and arithmetic" (p. iii). The authors went on to state, "Tests can play several different roles. One is as a means of public accountability" (p. 7). It seems as though the underlying concepts of NCLB have been around for quite some time.

The NCLB Act was yet another example of how this country stumbles through reform with a questionable political ideology and an educational accountability system that relies on imprecise "high-stakes assessments" for all children. We suggest strongly that you read the legislation, especially the portions on accountability, to gain a full understanding of the strength of the assault propagated against the unitary public school system.

Do not be fooled into thinking the intent of the law was noble based on the opportunistic name given to it by its creators. The entire act can be found online at www2.ed.gov/policy/elsec/leg/esea02/107-110.pdf. Reading the act with a critical eye helps illuminate overt and covert attempts to separate the public from public education through increased use of sanctions that ultimately lead to private, semiprivate, and corporate intrusion into public education.

A DEPARTMENT OF EDUCATION SECRETARY SPEAKS OUT

We cannot present a limited review of NCLB without first addressing that NCLB, in some ways, appears to be a classic bait-and-switch routine. Beyond the catchphrase "No Child Left Behind," seemingly plagiarized from the Children's Defense Fund's motto of "Leave No Child Behind," the Act has very little redeemable value in terms of improving the social welfare of children. It seems as if most supporters of the law never read the entire legislation and just latched on to the title. We now know from insiders in the Bush II administration that the law was not created to strengthen and grow the public education system.

Former assistant secretary for elementary and secondary education Susan Neuman stated in a June 8, 2008, *Time* magazine interview that some in the Bush administration and U.S. Department of Education viewed NCLB as a way to destroy public education so that the populace would support school choice, vouchers, privatization, and marketization; in effect, the law was being used as a Trojan horse to drive the wedge between the public and public education that would create the dual system (Wallis, 2008).

Neuman's statement might sound counterintuitive or even outlandish to those who view the USDOE as a pro–public school institution, but it stands up under scrutiny. For those readers who have tracked USDOE policy-making over the years it is clear that since the Reagan administration, the USDOE has become more antagonistic toward public education.

It was Reagan's secretary of education, Terrell Bell, who commissioned the *A Nation at Risk* report, and under the Clinton administration the USDOE, in 1995, started funding grants for charter school development. The Clinton administration handed out grants to help fund some of the 255 charter schools in operation in 1996. In 2000, President Clinton signed into law the New Markets and Community Renewal Initiative. That law is now being used by Wall Street banks and investment firms to pour hundreds of millions of dollars into the creation of charter schools in return for hundreds of millions in tax breaks and financing profits.

By 2005, the Bush II administration had swelled the number of charters to 3,344 with almost 700,000 students enrolled (USDOE, 2004, 2005). The Bush administration actively encouraged the proliferation of charter schools through statements made on the USDOE website. The now widely discredited Secretary Rod Paige and later, Margaret Spellings, set annual USDOE targets for additional growth of charter schools in operation and children served (USDOE, 2004, 2005).

The Bush administration and its DOE overplayed the benefits of charters in its various reports and on its website, and USDOE officials did not discuss any of the downsides such as de facto economic segregation, the siphoning of money from neighborhood public schools, and the lack of evidence supporting an empirical connection between charter schools and improved student achievement when comparing the achievement of similar students in traditional public schools (USDOE, 2004, 2005), all the while requiring schools to use data from empirically vapid standardized tests to drive their programs.

NCLB AND EMPIRICALLY FLAWED ACCOUNTABILITY

Whereas tests have long been used for diagnostic, formative (feedback for improvement), and summative (final grade) purposes, testing under NCLB was reduced in the new "educational reform" to demonstrate only a quantitative increase of tested student achievement on a narrow portion of a state's curriculum. The NCLB Act required all states to establish student *adequate yearly progress targets* (AYPTs) toward 100 percent student proficiency, an empirically unachievable goal, by 2014.

These proficiency targets must be explained in percentages of students meeting some arbitrarily identified score on standardized state exams in grades 3 through 8 and one year in high school in language arts, mathematics, and in some grade levels, science.

The percentages of students who must "pass" under NCLB are extreme indeed. The law called for 100 percent "proficiency" on statewide tests by 2014. According to then assistant secretary of elementary and secondary education under the Bush administration, Susan Neuman, no country on the face of the Earth has demonstrated the ability to achieve that mandate (Wallis, 2008). Robert Linn (2003) demonstrated that it would take 57 years for 100 percent of grade 4 regular education students to reach 100 percent proficiency in mathematics, 61 years for grade 8 students, and 166 years for grade 12 students (p. 6). Hardly scientifically based policy making.

Testing in America

Standardized testing in the United States has been a "way of school life" for almost 100 years. Beginning with the U.S. Army's development and use of the Alpha Test to screen for officer candidates during World War I, the practice moved quickly into the classroom. However, the NCLB reform movement brought about batteries of tests that tended to be state-designed (and with all the flaws you'd expect from amateurs), making testing more like "Trick-or-Treat" on Halloween. Key states such as Texas, California, Florida, Massachusetts, New York, Michigan, Arizona, Washington, and Oregon created assessments that allegedly measured student competence in a variety of subject areas.

These tests must be classified as being summative (a final grade), as they yield no information that can be used in a formative (feedback showing where and how to improve) or diagnostic fashion. There simply are not enough questions on these tests to be diagnostic in any one skill. And, under NCLB, national high-stakes testing on a yearly basis has become the norm.

Use of any single standardized test for making lifelong decisions for someone else is claimed to be unprofessional by most American educators. That point is strongly made in the *Standards for Educational and Psychological Tests* (1999) jointly endorsed by the American Educational Research Association (AERA), American Psychological Association (APA), and the National Council on Measurement in Education (NCME).

Other professional associations opposing wide-spread high-stakes testing include American Evaluation Association, the National Council for Teachers of English, the National Council for Teachers of Mathematics, the International Reading Association, the College and University Faculty Assembly for the National Council of Social Studies, the Association for Supervision and Curriculum Development, and the Alliance for Childhood. But these associations do not have a vote in the U.S. Congress or any state legislature.

Identical Standards on This Path

NCLB mandated that every child in every school in every state shall meet every standard. If that seems unrealistic, all we can say is, that's the law of the land. In sum, every child in the United States of America is to be on the same page on a given day at exactly High Noon. That the sponsors of NCLB, and now the Common Core State Standards and Race to the Top, ignored the past century's research on child growth and development is most obvious.

As a matter of note, no country on Planet Earth expects every child to master every standard. Ah, but we Americans have "World Class Standards" (wink, wink). But to be objective, let us examine data from the National Assessment of Education Progress (NAEP), arguably the best tests in the United States.

Accompanying the NAEP data tables is the Epstein/Piaget Child Growth and Development chart, showing the cognitive potential for children at varying ages and grades (2002). These data reflect the notion that children grow and develop as they mature. However, not all children of any age group will be at that level on the same month or even the same year.

Children develop at very different "speeds," which is one reason why tables 4.1 through 4.4 show a range of results. Some children mature cognitively earlier than others. For example, Piaget's Concrete Operations stage includes most students ages 7 through 11, but of course some students enter earlier or later, and others move to Formal Operations prior to age 11.

Examining the NAEP Data through Developmental Screens

Observe how from data in table 4.1 one could predict that 0 percent of the nine-year-olds would be able to master content at the NAEP 350 Advanced Level! This is evidence that can only be interpreted as over a 20-year period of time, no nine-year-olds are capable of mastering the higher level thinking items on the NAEP tests. Benjamin S. Bloom et al. (1954) initially categorized human cognition in six domains—knowledge, comprehension, application, analysis, synthesis, and evaluation/creation.

Knowledge includes recall of basic facts or information, whereas Comprehension means a student understands the meaning of the knowledge. The Application domain is where a student can apply the newly acquired information in a new situation. The Analysis domain requires a student look for motives, discrete parts, and inferences. The Synthesis domain is one requiring creativity, and the Evaluation/Creation domain requires a student to establish criteria for making judgments. One can equate the NAEP 350 Level with "Bloom's Taxonomy" domains of analysis, synthesis, and evaluation/creation, the so-called "higher-order" domains (Bloom, 1954).

Notice how the percentage of students scoring at the higher levels increases with chronological age from 1977 through 2008 (table 4.1). This supports our point about the relationship between cognitive development and achievement of NAEP standards and demonstrates the importance of setting standards and achievement targets based on cognitive development rather than political ideology. It also demonstrates clearly that one can create an education achievement crisis by simply mandating children achieve standards that are beyond normal cognitive developmental levels.

Conversely, observe the gradual decrease in fourth-grader percentages correct by moving from Levels 150 to 250. At NAEP Level 150, the percentages (correct) range from 91 to 96 percent. No question, these are concrete cognition problems, along with NAEP Level 250. One would predict the downward scores from the NAEP tabular descriptions of the cognitive levels. It appears that the critical level for fourth-graders is NAEP Level 250 or the equivalent of Bloom's Application Level (table 4.2).

Observe parallel patterns for 13- and 17-year-olds. These American youth do brilliantly at NAEP Level 150. Teachers and textbooks have long focused on this "knowledge" or recall level. As students are tested at the top three NAEP levels, there are fewer and fewer correct responses. One could argue, as would a naïve reformer, that American kids just don't work hard enough. There is some validity in that argument, but only up to a point. Here's the crucial point:

It will do little good to make 9- or 10-year-olds "work harder" if their cognitive development has not provided them with the needed cerebral connections for the level of the test. Or, if one were in the Lev Vygotsky (1978) camp of learning, then the conclusion would be that these children have not yet approached their *zone of proximal development*. This concept is defined as the difference between the intellectual level a child can reach on his or her own, and the level that can be reached with expert assistance—schooling.

Table 4.1. Percentages of Students Performing At or Above NAEP Mathematics Performance Levels, Ages 9, 13, and 17, for 1978, 1996, and 2008

Cognitive Expectation		Age 9			Age 13			Age 17		
Level	Description	% in 1978	% in 1996	% in 2008	% in 1978	% in 1996	% in 2008	% in 1978	% in 1996	% in 2008
350	Can solve multistep problems and use beginning algebra.	0	0	N/R	1	1	N/R	7	7	6
300	Can compute with decimals, fractions, and percents; recognize geometric figures; solve simple equations; and use moderately complex reasoning.	1	2	N/R	18	21	30	52	60	59*
250	Can add, subtract, multiply, and divide using whole numbers and solve one-step problems.	20	30	44*	65	79	83*	92	97	96*
200	Can add and subtract two-digit numbers and recognize relationships among coins.	70	82	89*	95	99	98*	100	100	N/R
150	Knows some addition and subtraction facts.	97	99	99*	100	100	N/R	100	100	N/R

Source: National Center for Education Statistics, National Assessment of Educational Progress (NAEP). *Report in Brief, NAEP 2008 Trends in Academic Progress.* Data for 2008 are from NCES 2009–479.
*Indicates that the percentage in 2008 is significantly different from that in 1978.

Table 4.2. Percentages of Students Performing At or Above NAEP Reading Performance Levels, Ages 9, 13, and 17, for 1978, 1996, and 2008

Level	Cognitive Expectation Description	Age 9			Age 13			Age 17		
		% in 1978	% in 1996	% in 2008	% in 1978	% in 1996	% in 2008	% in 1978	% in 1996	% in 2008
350	Can synthesize and learn from specialized reading materials.	0	0	N/R	0	1	13*	7	6	6
300	Can find, understand, summarize, and explain relatively complicated information.	1	1	N/R	10	14	63*	39	39	39
250	Can search for specific information, interrelate ideas, and make generalizations.	16	18	21*	58	61	94*	79	81	80*
200	Can comprehend specific or sequentially related information.	59	64	73*	93	93	N/R	96	97	N/R
150	Can carry out simple, discrete reading tasks.	91	93	96*	100	100	N/R	100	100	N/R

Source: National Center for Education Statistics, National Assessment of Educational Progress (NAEP). *Report in Brief, NAEP 1996 Trends in Academic Progress.* Revised 1998. NCES 98-530, Table 3, p. 11. Data for 2008 are from NCES 2009-479. *The Nation's Report Card.*

*Indicates that the percentage in 2008 is significantly different from that in 1978.

For children aged 9 or 10 years old, there is a cognitive limit, albeit not *fixed*, but definitely testable using the NAEP achievement levels. Michael Shayer and Philip Adey (1981) made a similar argument, stating, "In two studies, it was found that no evidence of formal thinking capacity could be found in children under the age of 10, no matter how clever they were." Clever in this regard meant extrapolating exceptionally high intelligence quotients or IQs in the 160 range. (See table 4.3.)

But what about the 13- and 17-year-olds? Cannot *raise-the-bar reformers* expect more from them? The answer from the NAEP data appears to be a *tentative yes*. Tentative in that 13-year-olds could do better at the NAEP 250 Level; however, there is little room for improvement among the 17-year-olds at the 250 Level, since they are already approaching the maximum score. There might be developmental limits for 13- and 17-year-olds when seeking improvement at the NAEP 300 and 350 levels. (See table 4.3.)

One might predict improved performances for 13- to 17-year-olds by adapting many of the instructional techniques shown to have positive effects on achievement. Thus, being more efficient with the use of time and utilizing more inquiry-oriented and active-teaching strategies, student achievement could improve at Levels 300 and 350. Yet cost-benefit analyses would be needed to justify the predicted modest gains in student achievement as a consequence of teaching more in-depth and less in breadth (e.g., applying the concepts of scope and sequence).

A scope chart would show what concepts or material would be taught at which grade level. The sequence chart would show how those learnings would be taught at each grade level. This curriculum technique is often called "Spiral Curriculum," since concepts are expanded at each grade level.

However, as presented in those tables, the data are irrefutable—not every child can achieve at the top levels on any NAEP test at any age! We present a detailed explanation of the various cognitive levels in table 4.4.

Adequate Yearly Progress and 100 percent Proficiency by 2014

Adequate Yearly Progress (AYP) is the "heart" of the accountability rewards and penalties clauses of the NCLB reform railroad job. While the actual calculations of AYP vary, the essence is that every year, every state must establish achievement "targets" (interesting war metaphor) for all schools and children in their respective jurisdiction. From 2002 to 2014, the target will be raised so that by 2014 every child, that is, 100 percent of all the kids, must meet the target.

If you agree with the concept, it is accountability at its finest. If you have ever taken a statistics or measurement course, you view the AYPTs as an illogical application of norm-referenced statistics. In norm-referenced tests, the statistics are designed so that 50 percent of the takers are

Table 4.3. Percentage of Students at Piaget's Cognitive Levels

Age	Grade	Intuition	Entry Concrete [a]	Advanced Concrete [b]	Entry Formal [a]	Middle Formal [b]	Ref.
5.5	P	78	22				J
6	K	68	27	5			A
7	1	35	55	10			A, W
8	2	25	55	20			A
9	3	15	55	30			A
10	4	12	52	35	1		S
11	5	6	49	40	5		S
12	6–7	5	32	51	12		S
13	7–8	2	34	44	14	6	S
14	8–9	1	32	43	15	9	S
15	9–10	1	15	53	18	13	S
16	10–11	1	13	50	17	19	S
16–17	11–12	3	19	47	19	12	R
17–18	12	1	15	50	15	19	R
Adult	—	20	22	26	17	15	R

Source: Herman T. Epstein, Personal communication, June 8, 1999. See also Epstein 2002.
[a]Children who have just begun to manifest one or two of that level's reasoning schemes
[b]Children manifesting a half dozen or more reasoning schemes
A—Arlin, P. Personal communication with H. T. Epstein.
J—Smedslund, J. (1964). *Concrete Reasoning: A Study of Intellectual Development.* Lafayette, IN: Child Development Publications of the Society for Research in Child Development.
R—Renner, J. W., Stafford, D. G., Lawson, A. E., McKinnon, J. W., Friot, F. E. & Kellogg, D. H. (1976). *Research, Teaching and Learning with the Piaget Model.* Norman: University of Oklahoma Press.
S—Shayer, M. & Adey, P. (1981). *Towards a Science of Science Teaching.* London: Heinemann.
W—Wei, T. D., et al. (1971). "Piaget's Concept of Classification: A Comparative Study of Socially Disadvantaged and Middle-Class Young Children." *Child Development* (42): 919–927.

below the median score and 50 percent above. For children in those states that use norm-referenced tests as their state-mandated exam, it is impossible to have all the test takers at the 99 percentile level. This is where statistical theory is totally ignored by the politicians who voted NCLB

Table 4.4.   Selected Concepts with Piagetian Descriptors Illustrating Concrete to Formal Development of a Child's Interaction with the World

Topic	Early Concrete	Late Concrete	Early Formal	Late Formal
Investigative Style	Unaided style does not produce models	Can serially order and classify objects	Is confused, needs interpretive model	Generates and checks possible explanations
Relationships	Can order a series but cannot make summarization	Readily uses the notion of reversibility	Can begin to use two independent variables	Reflects on reciprocal relationship between variables
Use of Models	Simple comparisons, one to one	Simple models: e.g., gearbox, skeleton	Deductive comparisons and models are taken as being true	Searches for explanatory model, uses proportional thinking
Categorizations	Objects are classified by one criterion: e.g., color, size	Partially orders and classifies hierarchically	Generalizes to impose meaning over wide range of phenomena	Abstract ideas generated, search for underlying associations
Proportionality	Needs whole sets to double or halve	Makes inferences from constant ratios and with whole numbers only	Makes inferences on ratio variables —Density = Mass/Volume	Knows direct and inverse relationship ratios
Mathematical Operations	Number is distinguished from size or shape	Works single operations but needs closure	Generalizes by concrete examples and accepts lack of closure	Conceives of a variable properly
Probabilistic Thinking	No notions of probability	Given equal number of objects knows there is 50/50 chance of one being drawn	Given set of objects can express chances in simple fractions	

Source: Michael Shayer and Philip Adey. *Towards a Science of Science Teaching: Cognitive Development and Curriculum Demand, 1981.* London: Heinemann. Abstracted from Table 8.1, pp. 72–78.

into law and by state education bureaucrats who zealously propagate the law.

Linn (2003) used the NAEP score trends for language arts and mathematics to show how statistically vapid the 100 percent proficiency requirement was from the outset. Linn used straight-line projections of
NAEP language arts and math trends to estimate the number of years it
would take students in grades 4 and 8 to achieve 100 percent proficiency
on the NAEP, assuming we could change human development to allow
all children to think at the formal operations stage by age 9.

Linn found it would take 57 years for grade 4 students to reach 100
percent mathematics proficiency, 61 years for grade 8 students, and 166
years for grade 12 students. It would take even longer for students in
those grade levels to reach 100 percent proficiency in reading (Linn,
2003).

Keep in mind that the NAEP achievement-level categories have been
criticized severely for being unrealistic and arbitrary (Pellegrino, Jones &
Mitchell, 1999). We use Linn's (2003) work to illustrate the unrealistic
expectations being placed upon the public school system and as additional evidence to support Neuman's statement in the June 8, 2008, issue of
Time magazine that many in the Bush administration saw NCLB as a way
to break the public schools and usher in greater fracturing of the unitary
system through privatization and choice.

Combinations and Permutations

NCLB required that all achievement data be reported for five different
groups. But the five groups are broken down into many smaller seg-
ments, making for hundreds of crucial calculations each school must face
each year. Paul Simon gave us over four dozen ways to leave your lover,
and George W. Bush and crew have given us "720 ways to flunk the
federal mandate."

Just stop and calculate all various combinations and permutations of
the groups that must pass all the tests: The odds are stacked. For example, there are only 27 different categories of children needing special
education, which includes six broad categories—intellectual, communi-
cative, sensory, behavioral, physical, and multiple (Ysseldyke and Algo-
zinne, 1995). Add to that the number of different racial and ethnic groups
that you have in the United States and the number expands.

Separate Measures for Subgroups

But let us be objective. NCLB requires schools and school districts to
report separate test achievement data for all the following 12 subgroups:
(a) economically disadvantaged; (b) White; (c) Black; (d) Native
American; (e) Hispanic; (f) Asian; (g) multiethnic; (h) special education;
(i) English language learners; (j) migrants; (k) all students; and (l) all
students except special education. Now multiply each of the 12 sub-

groups by "boys" and "girls," because the traits must also be reported by gender, and the number of reporting subgroups equals 24. But we are not done.

Scores must be reported for reading/language arts, mathematics, and science. That makes it three times 24, or 72 separate entries. Then an entry must be made for each grade level, 3 through 12, so 30 more variables are added. So 72 times 10 means that one needs a grid of potentially 720 reportable traits for a school district. In order to meet AYP, a school system must pass muster in each and every one of the 720 categories! (This, just when you thought creating spreadsheets was a snap.)

NAEP Results as Another Nail in the Unitary System Coffin

The NCLB Act also placed more credence in the National Assessment of Education Progress (NAEP) results as a way to "benchmark" state performance. As stated in an earlier chapter, NAEP is a mandatory national test given to representative samples of students in grades 4, 8, and 12 in private and public schools in each state.

The subjects tested are language arts, mathematics, U.S. history, geography, arts, civics, economics, science, and writing. Subjects are tested on a rotating basis every two to four years with language arts and mathematics occurring most frequently. In 2009 the U.S. Department of Education (USDOE) mandated that states place statewide NAEP result data on all school report cards directly next to statewide standardized test results.

There is a notion in the USDOE that statewide test results are overly inflated because states lowered their standards in response to NCLB's mandate of 100 percent proficiency. The USDOE's requirement to include national NAEP results for grade 4 and 8 students on the school report cards is meant to create doubt in the mind of the public about the difficulty of their state's test, because in most cases, the percentage of students rated as proficient on NAEP will be significantly lower than the percentage rated proficient on the statewide test.

In essence, the USDOE is setting up the NAEP to become the blueprint for the de facto national assessments. As we presented in the tables above, it is developmentally and empirically unreasonable to believe all students will score at the higher levels of the NAEP categories. The national standardized tests derive their proficiency categories from the NAEP. Therefore, there will always be a sizable portion of students who score at the "basic" level on the national tests, and that is physiologically normal.

The policy action of using NAEP results to benchmark state and national achievement was antagonistic to the NAEP design. The NAEP tests were designed to *sample* fourth-, eighth-, and twelfth-graders. The operational term is *"sample."* These tests were not designed for large-scale administration to every child in America, and they were not meant to act as proficiency benchmarks from which to compare or evaluate the difficulty or quality of state tests.

The statistical premise and theory under which NAEP assessments were designed call for specified small group sampling only. The idea that the NAEP will act as the de facto national test or the blueprint for such an instrument is a totally invalid use of the NAEP protocols. But beware, the Common Core State Standards initiative includes a national achievement test so we will endure the same problems and limitations of testing that we had with NCLB, although the research tells us such a system is broken.

There will be significant problems with linking national standardized test results to school improvement efforts at the state level as a way to evaluate gains and quality of standards or achievement: The NAEP achievement levels have never been validated and thus, the national test achievement levels will face the same problem. There is no empirical evidence to support the current national proficiency levels being set at their current cut-scores.

The USDOE recognized this problem with NAEP. According to the USDOE (2004), the NCES reports achievement levels as below *Basic*, *Proficient*, and *Advanced*. As provided by law, NCES, upon review of a congressionally mandated evaluation of NAEP, has determined that the achievement levels are to be used on a trial basis and should be interpreted and used with caution. However, both NCES and the National Assessment Governing Board (NAGB) believe that these performance standards are useful for understanding trends in student achievement (p. 198).

It seems contradictory to say that the NAEP levels should be used on a trial basis only and then turn around and use the NAEP achievement levels to make evaluations about state achievement and the overall effectiveness of the nation's public school system.

Pellegrino, Jones, and Mitchell (1999) conducted a congressionally mandated independent evaluation of the NAEP testing program. They stated that the proficiency levels and the way the National Assessment Governing Board (NAGB) sets the proficiency levels are fatally flawed: We recommend that the current model for setting achievement levels be abandoned. A new approach is needed for establishing achievement levels in conjunction with the development of new NAEP frameworks for assessments to be administered in 2003 and later (p. 175).

A new approach has not been developed for NAEP, and we are left years later with empirically bankrupt proficiency levels and proficiency-level-setting procedures. Ironically, the vendors of the national tests based on the CCSS are using the same process! Even the U.S. Congress recommended that the NAEP proficiency levels not be used to make important decisions about education. Pellegrino, Jones, and Mitchell (1999) found:

Congress stated that NAEP's student performance levels shall be used on a developmental basis until the commissioner of NCES determines, as a result of a congressionally authorized evaluation, that such levels are reasonable, valid, and informative to the public. Given the flawed current achievement-level-setting process, attendant concerns about the validity of the current achievement levels, and lack of proven alternatives, NAEP's current achievement levels should continue to be used on a developmental basis only. (p. 175)

Unfortunately, the NAEP performance levels have not been revised, the proficiency-setting procedure has not been improved, and the US-DOE continues to use the NAEP as the blueprint for a national standardized testing program. One might think that if the NAEP levels were in fact valid, then perhaps there should be examples where the vast majority of students around the world should be able to attain proficiency. This is not the case.

Phillips (2007) conducted a study that equated scores from the 2003 Third International Mathematics and Science Study (TIMSS) scores to the NAEP proficiency scales for grade 8. Phillips found that only five countries would have more than 50 percent of their students who attained average mathematics achievement on the TIMSS that could be categorized as proficient using the NAEP proficiency levels: Singapore, Korea, Hong Kong, Chinese Taipei, and Japan.

Less than 75 percent of the students in Singapore would be proficient using NAEP standards, and fewer than two-thirds of students in Korea, Hong Kong, Chinese Taipei, and Japan. Only 9 out of 38 nations would have a statistically significant higher average NAEP score than the United States.

On the grade 8 TIMSS science, only 9 out of 46 countries would have had statistically significant higher achievement on the NAEP than the United States. Thus it seems that most of the world's students would not be proficient on the NAEP mathematics or science tests at grade 8. Could the entire world's education systems be failing, or is there something invalid with the NAEP proficiency levels?

Central Control of the Democratic Institution

We find it amusing that the bureaucrats in the U.S. government, the government that oversees the most unique democratic experiment on the planet, has created a system to undermine that very democracy by dismantling the public school system. The NCLB Act, Common Core State Standards initiative, and Race to the Top amount to central control of the most important social institution for the preservation of a participative, locally controlled democracy.

No doubt that many of you are old enough to remember how well central control worked for the now-defunct Soviet Union, or at least you read about it in the history books—we hope. What may be amazing, perhaps tragicomic, is the central control double-speak in the following section, quoted directly from the NCLB.

> Nothing in this section shall be construed to alter or otherwise affect the rights, remedies and procedures afforded school or school district employees under Federal, State or local laws (including applicable regulations or court orders) or under the terms of collective bargaining agreements, memoranda of understanding, or other agreements between such employees and their employers. (115 STAT.1491)

The entire accountability section of NCLB violates at least the spirit, if not the legality, of the democratic rights or privileges of everyone employed in the public schools and those of the children. NCLB very conveniently sidesteps contract law, despite the language above. Mintrop and Sunderman (2009) observed:

> This new performance management system increases central control by top management, freezing out the mediating functions of the middle layers of the organization. In the political realm, this new approach to public administration increases the potential for a small group of centrally positioned elites to steer a whole system. (pp. 353–354)

Baines (2011) coined the centralization of the free and democratic public school system the "Stalinization of Education" and warned us of the deleterious effects. The similarities to NCLB, and now the plans for the CCSS and national testing, are eerily similar to those of the Soviet Union over 70 years ago:

> In many ways, Stalin's Five Year Plan amounted to a military takeover of Soviet schools, replete with the surrender of the pedologists, the conversion of teachers to the Communist party line, and the whole-scale politicization of schooling. The Five Year Plan forced Soviet schools to change from loosely-organized, largely locally-controlled, child-centered schools to tightly-governed, centrally-controlled, outcomes-focused schools. Of course, one of the problems with a militaristic orientation is that it often clashes with the delicate, immeasurable, exhausting work that goes along with helping a child develop into a fully realized adult. Openness, benevolence, spontaneity, tolerance, and intellectual skepticism might be attractive traits for a teacher, but they could cost a soldier his or her life. The American military today is strong, agile, and effective, but a militaristic orientation may not be optimal for educating young children. If pay-for-performance becomes a reality for teachers in America, as it looks like it will, the transformation from teacher as caretaker-nurturer to teacher as technician-soldier will be complete. Thus, the qualities of what constitutes a "good teacher" will be transformed utterly—from child-centered to curriculum-centered. (p. 4)

POINTS TO REMEMBER

At the federal level there is a need to examine the practicality, rationality, and lack of statistical logic in setting adequate yearly progress targets. The NCLB underlying accountability assumptions appear to be invalid. There are not adequate fiscal, human, and social resources to create 50 state systems of education that ensure 100 percent of all students passing one high-stakes test. Nor is there a comprehensive social system, aimed at blunting the deleterious influences of poverty, in place to support 100 percent of American students.

The NCLB Act and the continuation of its accountability system under the various waiver schemes, CCSS, and the ESEA reauthorization are simply making it impossible to show real student achievement, and therefore ultimately putting all public schools at risk of being sold to the lowest bidder. This should absolutely be "the path not taken."

As Sharon Nichols and David C. Berliner (2005) concluded, the No Child Left Behind Act is a "corrupting influence" on this noble American institution. Prior to NCLB, the schools were viewed as a moral pillar in our society. Opportunistic politicians and unknowing individuals and some so-called "education leaders" with little moral conviction and even less understanding of their profession's history and research are debasing that pillar.

A LOOK AHEAD

In the next chapter we connect some dots between the test-crazed policy environment, poverty, and the negative psychological effects of bad policy on children. We add up the costs of NCLB-style testing policies and wonder aloud if the costs to children and the unitary system of public education are worth it.

NOTE

The writers thank the *Clearing House* journal for permission to use lengthy excerpts in this chapter from author Orlich's "The No Child Left Behind Act: An Illogical Accountability Model" 78(1): 6–11, September/October 2004.

REFERENCES

American Educational Research Association, American Psychological Association & National Council on Measurement in Education (1999). Standards for educational and psychological testing, Washington, DC: American Educational Research Association.

Baines, L. (September 16, 2011). Stalinizing American education. *Teachers College Press*. Retrieved from www.tcrecord.org, ID Number: 16545.

Bass, F., Dizon, N. Z. & B. Feller. (April 18, 2006). Review of Test Results Finds Huge Loophole in Bush's No Child Left Behind Law. Associated Press.

Bloom, B. S., et al. (1954). *Taxonomy of Educational Objectives: The Classification of Educational Goals. Handbook 1: Cognitive Domain.* New York: David McKay.

Committee on Testing and Basic Skills. (1978). *Improving educational achievement.* Washington, DC: National Academy of Education.

Elementary and Secondary Education (ESEA) Act of 1965, Pub. L. No. 89-10, (1965).

Epstein. H. T. (2002). Biopsychological Aspects of Memory and Education. In: *Advances in Psychology Research* 11: 197–203.

Linn, R. L. (2003). 2003 Presidential Address. Accountability: Responsibility and Reasonable Expectations. *Educational Researcher* 32(7): 3–13.

Mintrop, H. & Sunderman, L. G. (2009). Predictable failure of federal sanctions-driven accountability for school improvement—and why we may retain it anyway. *Educational Researcher* 38(5): 353–361.

National Center for Education Statistics. (1998). *National Assessment of Educational Progress (NAEP). Report in Brief, NAEP 1996 Trends in Academic Progress.* Revised 1998. NCES 98–530.

National Center for Education Statistics, (1998; 2008). *National Assessment of Educational Progress (NAEP). Report in Brief, NAEP 1996 Trends in Academic Progress.* Revised 1998. NCES 98-530, Table 3, p. 11. Data for 2008 are from NCES 2009-479. *The Nation's Report Card.*

Nichols, S., & Berliner, D. C. (2005). *The Inevitable Corruption of Indicators and Educators Through High-Stakes Testing.* Tempe, AZ: Education Policy Research Unit, College of Education, Arizona State University. www.greatlakescenter.org/pdf/EPSL-0503-101-EPRU.pdf.

No Child Left Behind (NCLB) Act of 2001, Pub. L. No. 107-110, § 115, Stat. 1425 (January 8, 2002).

Pellegrino, J., Jones, L. & Mitchell, K. (Eds.). (1999). Grading the Nation's Report Card: Evaluating NAEP and Transforming the Assessment of Educational Progress. Washington, DC: National Academy Press.

Phillips, G. (2007) *Chance Favors the Prepared Mind: Mathematics and Science Indicators for Comparing States and Nations.* Washington, DC: American Institutes for Research.

Shayer, M. & Adey, P. (1981). *Towards a Science of Science Teaching: Cognitive Development and Curriculum Demand.* London: Heinemann.

United States Department of Education. (2004). FY 2004 performance and accountability report. USDOE: Author.www.ed.gov/about/reports/annual/2004report/index. html.

United States Department of Education. (2005). FY 2005 performance and accountability report. USDOE: Author.www.ed.gov/about/reports/annual/2005report/index. html.

Vygotsky, L. S. (1978). *Mind in Society: The Development of Higher Psychological Processes.* Chapter 6, Interaction between learning and development (79–91). Cambridge, MA: Harvard University Press.

Wallis, C. (June 8, 2008). No Child Left Behind: Doomed to Fail? *Time* magazine.

Ysseldyke, J. E. & Algonzzine, B. (1995). *Special Education: A Practical Approach for Teachers,* 3rd ed. Boston: Houghton Mifflin.

FIVE

The Path of High-Risk Implications for Public Education

A case might be made that we as a nation have been guided into reform by fear, mythology, and lies. American education reform has a four-century historical precedent. But the new "reforms" are a result of business interests and antidemocratic, anti–public school political forces that are prescribing increased student achievement of a narrow curriculum by imposing arbitrary and in some cases developmentally inappropriate standards for all students. In the meantime, instructional responsibilities are simply sloughed off to the classroom teachers.

To borrow from one popular political slogan: "Students and teachers, are you better off today than you were before federal and state coerced standards were mandated?" Or, "Administrators, have you been able to provide your teachers with the tools, support services, instructional materials, and training to reach more students as a result of state and federal mandated reform?"

Momentum for contemporary American school reform can be traced to the 1983 tract *A Nation at Risk* (NCEE, 1983). The antischool report rang the alarm bell, and educational reform is being driven by that good old psychological device—*fear*. *Global economic competition* is the "hobgoblin," and schools are now erroneously considered the exclusive engines for worker productivity. One must ask a rhetorical question: "Have the schools ever been assigned this role?"

In 1861, Herbert Spencer asked a parallel question: "What knowledge is of most worth?" in his book *Education: Intellectual, Moral and Physical*. Spencer answered with five educational purposes: self-preservation, meaningful work, familial support, social and political responsibilities, and worthy use of leisure time. The reform movement gains energy from political and profit-seeking capitalistic motivations that stress only mean-

71

ingful work and neglect all the others. (We are bold enough to suggest "cheap labor is what modern school 'reform' is really about.")

Scapegoating and fear appear to drive the current genre of educational legislation. In the years of 2002 and 2003, over 1,000 different bills were introduced in the 50 legislatures to "fix the schools." Somewhere along the way to fixing the schools, somebody—maybe everybody—forgot to ask, "What needs fixing?"

Rather than examining the underlying social factors of poverty, race, immigrants, non-English-speaking students, dysfunctional families, absenteeism, violence, and educational fads, the reform movement has simply degenerated into a single-minded high-stakes testing phenomena! Sure, we have educational problems. No social institution is perfect. And if you get a small enough sample, you can make any situation look "at risk." But who is really at risk now?

REFLECTING ON THE REAL RISKS

A child's socioeconomic background can be used as a predictor of high-stakes test success or failure. For example, Turnamian and Tienken (2012) demonstrated that by just knowing a community's percentage of lone parent households, the percentage of residents with at least a B.A. degree, and the percentage of economically disadvantaged children, one could predict district-level grade 3 state test scores in language arts and mathematics for 60 percent of the school districts in New Jersey. Maylone (2002) was able to do the same thing for high school test scores in Michigan.

These studies suggest that when policy makers and education bureaucrats use the results from high-stakes tests to make important decisions about educator quality and student learning, they are in fact penalizing poor children and their teachers for conditions over which these youngsters and adults have no control. Applying the *fairness doctrine*, this is a strong indictment, specifically against NCLB and, in general, all high-stakes tests—and the intuitive standards driving them.

What are some attributes of childhood poverty that negatively impact school outcomes? The first is inadequate nutrition. There is a definite relationship between malnutrition and cognitive dysfunction. Chronic vitamin B1 and B12 deficiencies have a demonstrated relationship to cognitive impairment (Beers and Berkow, Eds., 1999). Others include single-parent family structure and less access to life experiences that build sight vocabulary (Shim, Felner & Shim, 2001).

Poverty itself, the lack of money, is a key factor. The resource allocation for schools is directly related to property tax bases. Thus persons in poverty do not have the fiscal support to provide optimal learning environments for their children. State education bureaucrats provide funding to schools in impoverished communities, but that funding is for the act of schooling. It does little to ameliorate the environmental effects of living in poverty.

Jeffrey T. Fouts (2002) provided a most disturbing finding. By following individual children, he found that failure on the Washington Assessment of Student Learning (WASL), the state of Washington's high-stakes mandatory test at grade 4 used to satisfy the NCLB accountability requirements, begets failure in grades 7 and 10! That is, if students failed at grade 4, then they tended to fail in grades 7 and 10 also. More often the children that continue to fail the tests are children from poverty.

That sobering finding was actually suggested by Benjamin S. Bloom in 1964 in his seminal work *Stability and Change in Human Characteristics*. Bloom indicated that early learning deficits would require greater and more powerful instructional interventions later in schooling. To date, the only interventions provided by school reformers have been more testing and standardization. This leads directly to our next concept.

Learned Helplessness?

Poverty appears to be at least one condition that exacerbates the creation of averse educational consequences due to taking high-stakes tests. Failing students are apparently exhibiting characteristics of *learned helplessness*. As John Cosgrove (2000) notes, "Learned helplessness is a specific consequence of one particular form of psychological stress: being given an impossible task" (pp. 45–46).

Robert Sapolsky (1994) cites the research of Donald Hiroto and Martin E. P. Seligman showing how learned helplessness is a function of environmental conditions that are adverse. If children in grades 3, 4, or 5 have a very aversive experience with high-stakes tests, that is, fail to achieve the arbitrary standard that is set and receive the predictable negative consequences, then when they reach the middle school grades, they probably perceive passing that test as another impossible task.

Let us now invoke the theoretical construct of Abraham Maslow's (1954) "Hierarchy of Needs." Maslow constructed eight ascending psychological needs of which five are germane to our argument. Level 1 relates to basic physiological necessities such as food and water. Level 2 relates to safety needs, including shelter and security, while Level 3 describes the *belongingness* needs.

Level 4 is *Esteem*—the need to achieve, be competent, gain approval and recognition. Children who are informed that their test scores are *not meeting the standard* are being denied an element of *Esteem*. Being involuntarily subjected to standardized tests that include questions outside of the cognitive or life experience purview of some children by the police power of state governments produces the condition of *Learned Helplessness*.

Maslow's fifth level is *Cognitive*—the need to know, understand, and explore. It is claimed by the "reformers" that hundreds of thousands of children nationally have not entered that level—again based on test scores. With the *cognitive* need being contingent on the four basic physio-logical and psychological needs, it becomes apparent that poverty in general and learned helplessness specifically may be playing a more tragic role in student achievement than previously anticipated.

Children who live in impoverished environments with little chance to feel secure may be severely limited in their attempt to ascend beyond Levels 1 and 2 in Maslow's Hierarchy. This is because they must attend to their basic living necessities. Additionally, youth in these circumstances tend to be exposed to violence and remain at Level 2 since their safety needs are unmet. Progression to Level 5 is contingent on satisfying the first four levels.

It can be predicted that *stress* will develop as a consequence of a combination of learned helplessness and lack of meeting the first four needs in the Maslow Hierarchy (1954). *Depression* can set in when a stressful situation is perceived to be hopeless. This being the case, then no amount of testing will help children perform any better; probably they will perform worse.

The Path of Poverty

In 2012, the United Nations released *Child Poverty in Rich Countries: 2012*, The Innocenti Report Card No. 10. The Nordic countries had the lowest levels of child poverty in the "developed" countries of the world, primarily due to a highly subsidized spending of social benefits directly to families. The United States of America and Romania had the world's worst child poverty rates. For Romania the percentage was 25.5, and for the USA it was 23.1. The U.S. child poverty statistics place it last in the Organisation for Economic Co-operation and Development (OECD) group of industrialized countries.

The Innocenti report writers state that such disparity of wealth leaves many children, by no fault of their own, at a social disadvantage. The report also noted what we have already addressed in this chapter: that there is a close correlation between poverty and achievement on standardized tests. So, there you have it. Poverty is a powerful force in educational underachievement, and you will not find any major stroller on the reform path making that statement. And that includes Achieve, Inc.; the Business Roundtable; and a host of educational reform advocates.

One simply has to ask, "Why the silence?" One could speculate that Americans have been subtly conditioned and misled by Corporation USA into believing that childhood poverty is really not our social problem. This condition is an individual problem with slackers and lazy people who refuse to pull themselves up by their own bootstraps to achieve the American Dream.

Let us not forget the antipoverty messages carried by the nation's media during the 1970s through 1990s about all those "Welfare Queens." A nation that proclaims to defend democracy against all comers politely turns its back on its own poor. Aren't you proud of that?

The Path of Psychological Stress

We can look to the international scene to see where we are headed in terms of student stress and psychological issues. For example, on May 16, 2003, the day tenth-grade exam results were released in India, nine students killed themselves. "The inhumane stress put on children by the parents and teachers is the cause of this social evil—suicide," Indian state education minister Nalakathu Soopy told the Associated Press.

Thousands of students are believed to commit suicide over exams each year, but figures are sketchy, as some cases are not reported as exam-related. A study by *The Week* magazine in October 2002 estimated about 4,000 students take their lives each year in India (source: CNN News, June 30, 2003).

Granted, India is not the USA. But teenagers in the USA are now being subjected to the same "inhumane stress" as their Indian counterparts with NCLB, CCSS, national testing, and other recent accountability provisions. Teenage suicides are an unpleasant thought indeed, but current pressures brought on by high-stakes testing predict that these tragic acts of self-destruction will occur. Policy makers have subverted our longtime social contract with youth, and the corporate contract will undoubtedly precipitate the suicides of the more fragile youth as a result of that breach.

Another piece of evidence comes from the developmental cognitive levels table of Herman T. Epstein (2002; refer to table 4.3), who compiled national and international data on the cognitive development of children at varying age levels. These data were introduced in chapter 4 to support the argument that many of the tasks on state or nationally used tests are beyond the cognitive abilities of most fourth-graders.

The chart illustrates that at the fourth-grade level a mere 1 percent of children studied by Epstein were found to be at the entry level for mastering formal operational thinking. What may be more troubling or shocking is that only one-third of the adults can operate at the formal cognitive level. Now do you understand how easy it is for corporate and political charlatans to sell their educational snake oil?

Orlich's (2000 and 2005b) analysis of the state standardized tests from Washington showed it to be heavily weighted in the formal thinking area. But, as we have seen from Epstein, many teenagers cannot think formally at the mastery level. This leads to the proposition that *Learned Helplessness, stress, and depression* are the intended outcomes of the high-stakes test phenomenon. This has all the appearances of Sheila Tobias's

(1978) discussion of mathematics anxiety, which was closely aligned with learned helplessness. How ironic: the benefactors of this nation's "Greatest Generation" are now setting the stage to create its most "Learned Helpless Generation."

National Test Data and Family Income

The journal *Substance* (February 2002) published detailed tables showing results of the ACT and SAT test scores of college-bound seniors. The ACT scores are displayed showing family income in varying increments up to $100,000. In a very systematic progression, the ACT and SAT scores increased as family income increased.

The ACT composite score range low was 18.0 and the high 23.5, perfectly following the income increments. Identical data were derived for the SAT total, ranging from 872 to 1115, for the same income groups. Really, this is nothing new, as Allan Nairn (1980) reported similar relationships for the SAT in his study of family income and SAT results.

Orlich and Gifford computed a correlation coefficient of poverty to the 2004 SAT total (verbal plus mathematics) and obtained a value of 0.98. The correlation coefficient of parental income to the 2004 ACT composite scores was 0.99. Correlation coefficients for ethnicity and 2004 data for SAT total were 0.96 and for the ACT composite 0.96. For the SAT, 97 percent of the variance ($r^2 = .97$; $p < .001$) in test scores may be explained by family income of the test takers. Data for ACT mirror these findings closely. Coauthor Tienken (2010) replicated the SAT work for the 2008 scores and found similar results. (See table 5.1.)

Fair Test Examiner of fall 2005 presented 2005 college-bound seniors' scores on the ACT and SAT in similar fashion. The range of scores on the ACT composite were 17.9 to 23.5, while the SAT total score ranged from 884 to 1119. Computing 2005 SAT scores vs. family income, the SAT showed a correlation coefficient of .97, virtually identical to the 2004 correlation. The ACT followed a similar pattern in 2005. Additionally, ethnic differences ranged from 864 to 1091 on the 2005 SAT total, and 17.0 to 22.1 on the ACT composite.

Granted, the correlations were astoundingly high, but are not to be considered as "causal." Nevertheless, given the widespread use of tests to sort and/or classify students, the socioeconomic level, ethnic status, and social class of students need to be analyzed for apparent test bias by the educational community and policy makers. College and university admission officers need to factor in the above conclusions as they admit students and award financial aid or scholarships.

Table 5.1. The Correlation Between Family Income and SAT Results

Family Income	Reading	Math	Writing	Total	Diff.
Less than $20,000/year	434	456	430	1320	–
$20,000–$40,000/year	462	473	453	1388	+68
$40,000–$60,000/year	488	496	477	1461	+141
$60,000–$80,000/year	502	510	490	1502	+182
$80,000–$100,000/year	514	525	504	1543	+223
$100,000–$120,000/year	522	534	512	1568	+248
$120,000–$140,000/year	526	537	517	1580	+260
$140,000–$160,000/year	533	546	525	1604	+284
$160,000–$180,000/year	535	548	529	1612	+292
More than $200,000/year	554	570	552	1676	+356

Source: Tienken, C. H. (2010, Summer). Strong correlations. *AASA Journal of Scholarship and Practice* 7(2): 3–4.
Correlation between income and SAT score (Spearman Rho): .988**; .952**; .891**; .564*
* = p < .05; **= p <.001

THE PATH TO BANKRUPTCY AND THE COST OF SHIFTING EDUCATION REFORMS TO THE STATES

There is no free lunch, or dollars associated with NCLB. In May 2003, William J. Mathis published a must-read paper in the *Phi Delta Kappan.* We will briefly summarize his work that projects the costs for 10 states to fulfill matching requirements for NCLB. Table 5.2 shows a set of data indicating that nationally at least 55 percent more state money must be appropriated to meet the NCLB mandates.

Mathis cited the following interesting data. "New Hampshire will receive about $17 million in new money for new obligations of $126.5 million." That means the folks in the Granite State will put up $7.44 to gain $1.00 in federal funds. That is a bad investment by any measure. For example, New Hampshire gets a total of 3.3 percent of its K-12 budget from the federal government. (See table 5.2.)

Common Core Costs

The cost projections for the first seven years of implementation for the CCSS and national testing made by independent research firms exceed 15 billion dollars (Pioneer Institute, 2012) and could go even higher. The Pioneer Institute reported:

Chapter 5

Table 5.2. Projected Costs of Selected States to Meet NCLB Fiscal Mandates by 2014

State	Current Per Pupil Cost	Projected Per Pupil Cost	Percent of New Revenue Needed	NCLB New Money to State	New State Fiscal Obligations
Indiana	$5,468	$7,142	31%		
Maryland		$9K–$12K	34%–49%		$1.3 billion
Montana	$4,471	$6K–$8K	34%–80%		
New Hampshire				$17 million	$126.5 million
Nebraska	$5,600	Up to $12K	45%		
New York					$2.9 billion
South Carolina	$4,970	$9,182	84%		
Texas			35%		$6.9 billion
Vermont			15.5%	$51.6 million	$158.2 million
Wisconsin	$8,241	$11,121	35%		
All 50 States			55%		

Source: William J. Mathis. (May 2003). No Child Left Behind Costs and Benefits. *Phi Delta Kappan* 84(9): 679–686. Reprinted with permission.

> Over a typical standards time horizon of seven (7) years, we project Common Core implementation costs will total approximately $15.8 billion across participating states. This constitutes a "mid-range" estimate that only addresses the basic expenditures required for implementation of the new standards. It does not include the cost of additional expensive or controversial reforms that are sometimes recommended to help students meet high standards, such as performance-based compensation or reduced class sizes. (p. 1)

Not so astonishingly, most state education bureaucrats did not even anticipate how much full implementation will cost:

> Implementation of the Common Core standards is likely to represent substantial additional expense for most states. While a handful of states have begun to analyze these costs, most states have signed on to the initiative without a thorough, public vetting of the costs and benefits. In particular, there has been very little attention to the potential technology infrastructure costs that currently cash-strapped districts may face in order to implement the Common Core assessments within a reasonable testing window. (p. 26)

We need to examine the actual costs to the states alone to meet the accountability condition of NCLB and the CCSS and national testing.

How much has been spent already on this folly and how much will be wasted in the future? Obtaining state test costs data proved to be a difficult search, as the studies about state costs do not use the same definitions. *Our definition is what does the test alone cost, excluding indirect costs — teacher time, school days missed.*

The new national tests will raise the stakes even more in terms of spending. Over $300 million has already been spent on developing the next generation of assessments, and we predict those will look and "behave" strikingly similar to the tests we already force upon students. Although they might look shiny and new because most will be delivered via computer (another extra cost not discussed by bureaucrats), the technical characteristics will be no better, and the susceptibility of the results to be skewed by students' socioeconomic status will remain.

Essentially, we get the same type of tests we have today; we just spend over 300 million more dollars to change the name. But all this has been reported before. The players are the same this time around, and the game plan is unchanged. Why should anyone expect anything different?

For example, one year after the signing of NCLB, several investigative reports followed the money trail from the taxpayers to NCS Pearson. Writing in the *Minneapolis-St. Paul Business Journal* of March 3, 2003, Benno Groeneveld reported that NCS Pearson, which is a subsidiary of London-based Pearson PLC, reported a revenue increase of 42 percent in 2002, compared to 2001.

Ronnie Lynn (June 18, 2003) reported that in the state of Utah the costs for any basic-skills tests would range from $5 million to $7 million per year. Neighboring state Colorado reported spending $67 million between 1997 and 2003 for its CSAP exit test. Karen Rouse (August 2, 2004) explained that Colorado spent $14.85 million on testing a year. New Jersey's testing contract with Measurement Inc. amounted to approximately 29 million dollars a year to meet the NCLB mandates.

Reasonable estimates put the testing costs between $15 and $33 per student per year. In the USA, we have about 50 million children enrolled in K-12 schools. There are approximately 34 million in grades K-8 and about 14.5 million in grades 9-12. For the sake of computing a test cost, let us assume equal numbers in each grade level, or about 4 million in each grade. Federal law requires that we must test every child in grades 3 through 8, making six grades, and then grade 10 in high school. That's seven grades of testing total.

Those numbers compute to about 28 million children tested every year. Let us use the midpoint between published estimates of $15 and $33 per child per test or $24 per student. We multiply 28 million students by $24 per student and the sum equals $672 million per year for tests! Now we are talking real money. In 10 years, the magic estimated number jumps to $6.72 billion! No matter what the assumptions or definitions, the testing companies are benefiting very well, thank you. And they have to love NCLB, CCSS, and the national testing mandates.

Gerald W. Bracey (2005) analyzed several cost factors associated with NCLB and how there is a very apparent and substantial shifting of financial resources from the public sector to private sector companies. In his summary, just accounting for (1) tests, (2) supplemental educational services, and (3) curricula oriented toward the NCLB standards, he could account for over $5 billion. The cash flow to corporations is indeed a tidy windfall.

Calculating the Social Costs of Centralized and Standardized Accountability

In the business sector, financial statements often carry the category of "goodwill costs," which refer to the excess of a purchase price over the fair market value. That same category is now applied to NCLB and the host of high-stakes tests that permeate the landscape of reform. A more insidious factor—the social costs—has been identified by Sharon Nichols and David C. Berliner.

In a report titled *The Inevitable Corruption of Indicators and Educators through High-Stakes Testing* (2005), these researchers provide nationally gathered evidence to support Campbell's Law (1976). Campbell explained that "The more any quantitative social indicator is used for social decision-making, the more subject it will be to corruption pressures and the more apt it will be to distort and corrupt the social processes it is intended to monitor" (p. 49).

During the period of 2004–2005, Nichols and Berliner systematically monitored hundreds of news stories and research papers in America related to high-stakes testing as a hallmark of school reform. They found 10 categories of corrupting effects on high-stakes testing.

High-stakes tests simply corrupt and distort the educational processes. The 10 corrupting findings illustrate the exorbitant social costs being extracted that can never be repaid: (1) Administrator and Teacher Cheating; (2) Student Cheating; (3) Exclusion of Low Performance Students from Testing; (4) Misrepresentation of Student Dropouts; (5) Teaching to the Test; (6) Narrowing the Curriculum; (7) Conflicting Accountability Ratings; (8) Questions about the Meaning of Proficiency; (9) Declining Teacher Morale; (10) Score Reporting Errors.

Speaking of social costs, this is an opportune moment to add a postscript and reflect on Michael Harrington's (1962) *The Other America: Poverty in the United States*. His examination of the nation's conscience appeared at a time when we were celebrating the achievements of post World War II. Harrington argued and provided substantive data that several millions of Americans were trapped in a culture of poverty. President John F. Kennedy was profoundly influenced by this work, which led to his own "war on poverty." Of course, mainline politicians viewed

Harrington's work as simply a socialist's view and not really germane to mainstream Americans.

E. J. Dionne, Jr. (2000) observed that Harrington had great impatience with capitalism's tendency to privatize success while socializing failure. Private enterprise produces what sells in the marketplace. The government is stuck with dealing with tough social issues and problems, not addressed in the private sector. Dionne's observation is very pertinent to NCLB. Politicians realize that if the public schools' success stories continue, people may well begin to think at a higher level and see through the rhetorical nonsense that is amply expressed in accountability provisions of NCLB.

Let us add what has been a previously undiscussed analysis of the NCLB accountability provisions. Charles Pekow (2006) wrote that inspectors are to check for almost 600 compliance measures on all agencies that are affected by NCLB. The Office of Inspector General (OIG) at the Department of Education had identified 588 requirements needed for Title I, Part A of NCLB. None of the state guides include all 588, and even the Department of Education's guides only include 360 of them. So if you thought the discussion on indirect costs and unfunded mandates was a little suspicious, be advised your suspicions are not unfounded.

Sleep well tonight knowing that your school district will be submitting reports and certifications galore. What began as a test-makers' relief bill has truly evolved into an accountants' employment act. Do you now understand the gravity and sheer madness of the political nonsense that is being perpetrated on the land as a measure to improve the public schools?

POINTS TO REMEMBER

Yong Zhao (2012), one of our country's leading thinkers on how education can facilitate or inhibit innovation and creativity in students, explained the disastrous effects that centralization has on entrepreneurship in countries that suffocate their students' creativity and innovativeness. He cautions us all by stating that once a country goes over the edge of standardization and centralization with the use of a narrow curriculum enforced by a high-stakes national test, it will be hard to ever return to more innovating and decentralized forms of schooling.

A LOOK AHEAD

In the next chapter we dive further into the belly of the testing beast to uncover the flawed technical characteristics and less-than-stellar results of high-stakes testing policies. We then present some statistical evidence of the strong link between money and test scores.

NOTE

A substantial section of this chapter was reproduced from "The Relationship of Poverty and Test Scores," which was authored by D. C. Orlich and G. Gifford and published by *Leadership Information*, Summer 2005, copyright by School Information and Research Services, Olympia, Washington, and is reprinted with their permission.

REFERENCES

Beers, M. H. & Berkow, R. B. (Eds.). (1999). *The Merck Manual of Diagnosis and Therapy*, 17th ed. Rahway, NJ: Merck, Sharpe and Dohme Research Laboratories.

Bloom, B. S. (1964). *Stability and Change in Human Characteristics*. New York: John Wiley & Sons, Inc.

Bracey, G. W. (2005, June). *No Child Left Behind: Where Does the Money Go?* Tempe, AZ; College of Education, Arizona State University, Education Policy Research Unit, epsl-0506-114, EPRU.

Campbell, D. T. (1976, December). *Assessing the Impact of Planned Social Change*. The Public Affairs Center, Dartmouth College, Hanover New Hampshire, USA.

CNN Student News. (2003, July 1). India's Summer Heat Comes with Rash of Student Suicides. Retrieved at: cnn.com/2003/EDUCATION/06/30/india.student.suicides.ap/index.html.

Cosgrove, J. (2000). *Breakdown: Facts about Stress in Teaching*. New York: Routledge Falmer.

Dionne, E. J. Jr. (2000, March 31). Michael Harrington's "America Can" Reflects an Optimism about America's Social Possibilities That Needs to Be Rekindled. *Washington Post*.

Epstein, H. T. (2002). Biopsychological Aspects of Memory and Education. In: *Advances in Psychology Research* 11: 197–203.

Fair Test Examiner. (2005, Fall). University Testing: Latest SAT, ACT Results Flat, 19(4): 4–5.

Fouts, J. T. (2002, April). *The Power of Early Success: A Longitudinal Study of Student Performance on the Washington Assessment of Student Learning, 1998–2001*. Lynnwood, WA: Washington School Research Center, Research Report #1.

Groeneveld, B. (2003, May 4). NCS Pearson 2002 Revenue, Profits Up. Minneapolis–St. Paul: *The Business Journal*, p. 1.

Harrington, M. (1962). *The Other America: Poverty in the United States*. Baltimore: Penguin Books.

Krashen, S. (2002, February). Poverty Has a Powerful Impact on Educational Attainment, or, Don't Trust Ed Trust. *Substance* 27(6): 3.

Lynn, R. (2003, June 18). High School Exit Exam in Peril. *The Salt Lake Tribune*, p. B-1.

Maslow, A. (1954). *Motivation and Personality*. New York: Harper.

Mathis, W. J. (2003, May). No Child Left Behind Costs and Benefits. *Phi Delta Kappan* 84(9): 679–686.

Maylone, N. (2002). *The relationship of socioeconomic factors and district scores on the Michigan educational assessment program tests: An analysis*. (Unpublished doctoral dissertation). Eastern Michigan University.

Nairn, A. (1980). *The Reign of ETS: The Corporation That Makes Up Minds*. Washington, DC: Allan Nairn and Associates.

National Commission on Excellence in Education. (1983). *A Nation at Risk: The Imperative for Educational Reform*. Washington, DC: Author.

Nichols, S. & Berliner, D. C. (2005). *The Inevitable Corruption of Indicators and Educators Through High-Stakes Testing*. Tempe, AZ: Education Policy Research Unit, College of Education, Arizona State University. www.greatlakescenter.org/pdf/EPSL-0503-101-EPRU.pdf.

Office of State Superintendent of Public Instruction. Olympia: Contract with Pearson Educational Measurement, dated May 5, 2004, $70,800,000.00.

Office of State Superintendent of Public Instruction. Olympia: Contract with Riverside Publishing Company, dated September 20, 2001, $61,673,910.00.

Orlich, D. C. (2000). A Critical Analysis of the Grade Four Washington Assessment of Student Learning. *Curriculum in Context* 27(2): 10–14.

Orlich, D. C. (2005, March 15). *The WASL: A Critical Report to Interested Citizens of the State of Washington.* Pullman, WA: Washington State University, unpublished report circulated to every member of the Washington Legislature. (b)

Orlich, D. C. & Gifford, G. (2005, Summer). The Relationship of Poverty to Test Scores. *Leadership Information* 4(3): 34–38. (a)

Pekow, C. (2006). Federal Offices Disagree on Monitoring Under NCLB. *Grants for K-12 Hotline,* 18(10): 7, May 25, 2006; Boston: Quinlan Publishing.

Phelps, R. (2002, February). Estimating the Costs and Benefits of Educational Testing Programs. Education Consumers Consultants Network. Retrieved from www.education-consumers.com/briefs/feb2002.shtm.

Pioneer Institute. (2012). National Cost of Aligning States and Localities to the Common Core Standards. Author.

Rouse, K. (2004, August 2). CSAP Scores Due: Tab Sparks Debate. *The Denver Post,* p. A-1.

Sapolsky, R. (1994). *Why Zebras Don't Get Ulcers.* New York: Freeman and Co.

Shim, M. K., Felner, R. D. & Shim, E. (2000, April). *The Effects of Family Structures on Academic Achievement.* Paper presented at the Annual Meeting of the American Educational Research Association, New Orleans, LA.

Spencer, H. (1891). *Education: Intellectual, Moral and Physical.* New York: D. Appleton and Company. (Originally published in 1861.)

Tienken, C. H. (2010, Summer). Strong Correlations. *AASA Journal of Scholarship and Practice,* 7(2): 3–4.

Tobias, S. (1978). *Overcoming Math Anxiety.* New York: Norton.

Turnamian, P. & Tienken, C. H. (2012). *Use of Community Wealth Demographics to Predict Statewide Tests Results in Grade 3.* Paper presented at the National Council of Professors of Educational Administration Conference, Kansas City, MO, August 9, 2012.

UNICEF. (2005). *Child Poverty in Rich Countries, 2005.* Innocenti Report Card No. 6. Florence, Italy: UNICEF Research Centre. Retrieve at www.unicef.org/irc.

Zhao, Y. (2012). *World Class Learners: Educating Creative and Entrepreneurial Students.* Thousand Oaks, CA: Corwin Press.

SIX

High Stakes, Low Quality

It is clearer now that the modern school reform movement, the movement aimed at actually birthing a dual, two-tiered system of education in the United States, will use high-stakes testing, whether at the state level or national level as proposed by Council of Chief State School Officers (CCSSO), through the enactment the Common Core State Standards initiative, as the driving force to create the crisis in public education (CCSSO, 2009). The school accountability foundation is built on the assumption that one high-stakes test can determine a child's, school's, or school district's future. What data support or negate that assumption?

The Center on Education Policy published its analysis of state tests in *State High School Exit Exams: Put to the Test* (Gayler et al., 2003). The authors list data from 24 states showing the number of students passing the respective high school exit examinations. The range of subgroup passing percentages varied from 4 percent to 96 percent. But not one state could show any subgroup with 100 percent passing!

CAN WE TRUST THE TESTS?

Several researchers have analyzed selected state tests to illustrate innate problems. For example, Robert Linn and Carolyn Haug (2002) examined Colorado school-level test scores over a four-year period and concluded the following:

> The performance of successive cohorts of students is used in a substantial number of states to estimate the improvement of schools for purposes of accountability. The estimates of improvement, however, are quite volatile. This volatility results in some schools being recognized as outstanding and other schools identified as in need of improvement simply as the result of random fluctuations. It also means that strate-

gies of looking to schools that show large gains for clues of what other schools should do to improve student achievement will have little chance of identifying those practices that are most effective. On the other hand, schools that are identified as 'in need of improvement' will generally show increases in scores the year after they are identified simply because of the noise in the estimates of improvement and not because of the effectiveness of the special assistance provided to the schools or pressure that is put on them to improve. (p. 35)

Tienken (2008a) reviewed the tests used in grades 4, 8, and 11 in New Jersey and found vast differences in scores between students eligible for free lunch and those not eligible (poor versus more affluent). The review also demonstrated that the results from New Jersey's statewide assessments possess sizable amounts of error in the reported individual student scores. Individual student results from New Jersey's state tests can contain 6 to 13 scale-score points of error. New Jersey uses a "hard and fast" proficiency cut score of 200 out of a possible 300 scale score points.

Tienken found the hard and fast proficiency cut score combined with the fact that the New Jersey education bureaucrats either willingly do not account for the error or do not know how to overcome it in reported individual results inherently creates a situation in which students can be labeled as not proficient when in fact they are, but their true score is masked by the unaccounted-for error.

Similarly, Linda Darling-Hammond (2003) reported that doubt must be cast on state test gain scores because in Texas, students showed gains on the state-mandated assessment, but did not make comparable gains on national standardized tests or the Texas college entrance test.

Using an effect size measurement and Cohen's (1988) nominal definitions, Orlich (2003) found no effect, that is, no positive impact on yearly student achievement as a consequence of the four years of administration of the Washington Assessment of Student Learning (WASL). However, over a four-year period, a small effect, an insignificant gain does emerge. The effect size statistic is based on a normal distribution of scores. The larger the effect size, the greater the student gains. In Washington State, the gains were negligible in a year-to-year comparison.

The results of Orlich's study parallel the findings of Amrein and Berliner (2002a), who analyzed the consequences of 18 states with high-stakes tests. They reported that in 17 of the 18 states, student learning remained at the same level as it was before the policy of high-stakes tests was instituted. They concluded that high-stakes tests might actually worsen academic performance and exacerbate dropout rates. The affective dimensions of high-stakes tests should be of great concern to policy makers and educators alike. In a separate study of 28 states with high-stakes tests, Amrein and Berliner (2002b) concluded that these tests do little to improve student achievement.

Haney (2002) observed a "randomness" of school scores on the Massachusetts high-stakes test. That is, scores went up and down yearly, almost in a random manner similar to the Colorado findings. Braun (2004) cautioned that with all the variations in selecting and analyzing national test data, all conclusions about high-stakes tests and their impact on student achievement might be tentative at best. And Wilson (1999) concluded that construct validity is insufficient for assuming large-scale educational assessment internal validity. That is, these high-stakes tests may not be testing what they are intended to test.

REVIEW OF HIGH SCHOOL EXIT EXAMS AS AN EXAMPLE OF A BANKRUPT REFORM STRATEGY

One influence of 30 years of increased federal and state pressure to pursue assessment-driven education policies has been an increased use of high school exit exams. Broadly defined, a high school exit exam is any statewide standardized test given to all high-school students in a specified high school grade or at the end of specified courses, such as Algebra II or Biology, in which the results become the basis for a judgment about whether students can graduate high school with a standard diploma, not graduate, or receive a lesser diploma.

State education bureaucrats began to use high school exit exams as a policy lever to effect change in the public school system in Virginia. The SEA and state board of education in that state created a "minimum competency" test required for high school graduation (Sanger, 1978). In 1979, the New York SEA instituted a similar basic competency testing scheme for students in the ninth grade.

By 2001, prior to President George W. Bush signing the NCLB Act, 18 SEAs required public school youth pass a standardized statewide exit exam for graduation (Education Commission of the States, 2008). As of 2012, more than 50 percent of the SEAs required youth pass a standardized statewide test in at least Language Arts (LA) and mathematics to receive a standard high school diploma.

An overarching problem with state-mandated high school exit exams is that the results from all statewide tests of academic skills and knowledge at all grade levels have technical flaws that should restrict bureaucrats and school administrators from using the results as the only deciding factor to make life-changing decisions about individual students, such as whether a student graduates high school (American Education Research Association [AERA], American Psychological Association [APA] & National Council on Measurement in Education [NCME], 1999; Joint Committee on Testing Practices [JCTP], 2004). The limitations of the reported test results for individual students do not support the potential negative social and educational consequences raised by their use as a high school graduation requirement (Tienken, 2011).

Some unintended consequences of using only high school exit exam results as a decision point can include students being retained in grade, increased chances of economically disadvantaged students not completing high school (Borg, Plumlee & Stranahan, 2007), or placement in low-level course sequences (increases the chances of not completing high school). Other consequences include not receiving a standard high school diploma or being denied graduation altogether (e.g., Booher-Jennings, 2005; Burch, 2005).

All of the potential consequences listed cost taxpayers more money in the long term because of the depressed earnings of those who do not attain a high school diploma. Levin found that reduced employment earnings result in lower local, state, and federal tax receipts and lower earners also correlate with higher public medical costs, greater rates of incarceration, and greater use of the welfare system (Levin, 2009).

A specifically troublesome problem with results from all state tests, especially those used as graduation gatekeepers, is conditional standard error of measurement (CSEM) and its effect on individual test-score interpretation. The reported results for individual pupils might not be the true score.

The CSEM is an approximation or estimate of the amount of error one must consider when interpreting a test score at a proficiency cut-point (Harville, 1991). One can think of as the margin of error reported in political polls (e.g., + or – 3 points). The individual student-level results from all the state standardized tests have a margin of error. The CSEM helps to describe how large that margin of error is and how much the reported test results might differ from a student's theoretical true score (Tienken & Rodriguez, 2010).

For example, if a student receives a reported scale score of 198, and there are + or – 8 scale-score points of CSEM, then the possible true score could reside within the range of 190 to 206. Furthermore, if that state's proficiency cut score is 200, like it is in New Jersey, then the student is categorized as *not proficient* or failing if the SEA does not account for CSEM somehow in its calculations for individual students, even though the student scored within the CSEM band. This is especially troubling when bureaucrats and school administrators use a single test score to determine if a youth can graduate high school (Tienken, 2011).

If education bureaucrats within state agencies and legislators do not provide policy safeguards for the CSEM, then some percentage of students might be wrongly denied a standard high school diploma, when in fact they passed the exit exam. For example, based on information from the 2009 state test technical manual, about 9,500 New Jersey high school youth scored within the error range of the spring administration of their mathematics exit exam's CSEM at the proficiency cut score.

That means up to 9,500 students were potentially categorized as "not proficient" and forced to take remedial course work, retake the test, and/or participate in an alternative high school assessment process. These students lost out on valuable electives or other potentially rewarding school experiences.

Similarly, almost 54,000 students in California scored within the CSEM margin of error on their November 2006 LA exit exam. This happens in every state on every high-stakes test, not just those given in high school. The reported student-level scores are not the true scores, yet education bureaucrats and school administrators make determinations about graduation eligibility as if scores were error free (Tienken, 2011).

Standards for Education Testing

The authors of *Standards for Educational and Psychological Testing* (AERA, APA & NCME, 1999) developed specific standards and recommendations for test developers, test takers, and those who use test results to make decisions about children. The standards and recommendations address issues related to test construction, fairness in testing practices, appropriate documentation of technical characteristics of tests, and other important assessment topics.

Statements related to measurement error appear in Part I and Part III of the *Standards* (AERA, APA & NCME, 1999). For example, the authors of the *Standards* stated:

> Measurement error reduces the usefulness of measures. It limits the extent to which test results can be generalized beyond the particulars of a specific application of the measurement process. Therefore, it reduces the confidence that can be placed in any single measurement. (p. 27)

The authors of the *Standards* suggest strongly that test score error and other threats to precision be reported. The authors wrote, "The critical information on reliability includes the identification of the major sources of error, summary statistics bearing on the size of such error" (p. 27). Also, "Precision and consistency in measurement are always desirable. However, the need for precision increases as the consequences of decisions and interpretations grow in importance" (p. 30). The authors provided a rationale as to why test developers and users (i.e., SEA personnel) must report the CSEM at the cut score levels of their tests:

> Mismeasurement of examinees whose true scores are close to the cut score is a more serious concern. The techniques used to quantify reliability should recognize these circumstances. This can be done by reporting the conditional standard error in the vicinity of the critical value. (p. 30)

Several standards for test-score precision in high-stakes contexts exist (AERA, APA & NCME, 1999) that education bureaucrats, policy makers, and school administrators can use to guide high-stakes testing policy and decision making. Table 6.1 includes the applicable macro-standards, statements, and paraphrased recommendations. Authors of the *Standards* provide overall guidance on interpretation and score precision, "The higher the stakes . . . the more important it is that the test-based inferences are supported with strong evidence of technical quality" (p. 139).

Another standard, 7.9, seems especially poignant. The authors wrote, "When tests or assessments are proposed for use as instruments of social, educational or public policy, . . . users . . . should fully and accurately inform policy-makers of the characteristics of the tests" (p. 83). The *Standards* (AERA, APA & NCME, 1999) provide guidance about the influence of CSEM on construct validity related to the potential negative social and educational consequences for children. The *Standards* call clearly for test developers and users of test results to recognize CSEM as a factor that can influence score interpretation.

More National Study Results

Tienken (2011) conducted a nonexperimental, descriptive, cross-sectional study to (a) investigate the precision of the test results received from high school exit exams and to investigate the possible consequence of using those results for high-stakes decisions about students. Although

Table 6.1.   Standards for Educational and Psychological Testing (AERA, APA & NCME, 1999) Related to Test-Score Precision and Conditional Standard Error of Measurement

Standard	Standard Statement	Recommendations
2.2	"The standard error of measurement, both overall and conditional . . . , should be reported . . . in units of each derived score." (p. 31)	The *CSEM* is important in high school exit exam situations due to the consequence of imprecision.
5.10	"Those responsible for the testing programs should provide appropriate interpretations. (They) should describe . . . the precision of the scores, common misinterpretations of test scores." (p. 65)	Score precision should be illustrated by error bands or potential score ranges for individual students and should show the *CSEM*.
6.5	"When relevant for test interpretation, test documents ordinarily should include item level information, cut scores . . . the *SEM*." (p.69)	The *SEM* should be reported.

Source: Tienken, C. H. (2011). Structured Inequity: The Intersection of Socio-Economic Status and the Standard Error of Measurement of State Mandated High School Test Results. In B. Alford (Ed.). *NCPEA Yearbook* (pp. 257–271). Ypsilanti, MI: Proactive Publications.

the results reported are for high school exit exams, similar results were also found during a national review of all the state-mandated grade 8 tests in use between 2002–2008 and the grade 3, 4, and 8 tests used in New Jersey (Tienken, 2008a, 2008b).

Table 6.2 lists the name of each state, the most recently reported or approximate CSEM at the proficiency cut-point for the LA and mathematics portions of the high school exit exam, the number of opportunities to take and pass the exam, method used to address the presence of CSEM, whether the state used a "hard and fast" cut score (e.g., did not allow for a range of scores at the proficiency cut-point), and the number of students potentially affected by CSEM.

The range of CSEM at the proficiency cut-point for LA and/or mathematics tests given between 2004 and 2008 was 3.24 on the Idaho mathematics exit exam to 39 scale-score points on the Texas mathematics exit exam. Hence, the true math scores for Texas students can be + or − 39 points from the reported test score. The actual size of the error is less of a concern because each state uses a hard and fast cut score. Therefore, even one scale-score point of CSEM can cause misinterpretation and miscategorization of student performance.

The most common way that SEAs attempted to overcome CSEM was to provide multiple testing options. Every SEA provided students at least two opportunities to take and pass the standard high school exit exam. The mode was three testing opportunities. None of the SEAs reported policies that averaged students' scores from multiple testing opportunities to form a single score on a specific test (e.g., LA or math) to determine proficiency (Tienken, 2011).

Almost 60 percent of the SEAs did not provide information about how or if they accounted for CSEM in individual student test results. Only one SEA included a visual CSEM band on student reports. None of the SEAs accounted for the CSEM by awarding the student the theoretical higher score, the score at the top end of the CSEM band, even though SEA personnel know the CSEM exists (Tienken, 2011).

Nationally, Tienken (2011) estimated that 118,111 students were potentially denied a passing score on their state's high school exit exam in language arts and an estimated 114,391 students were denied a passing score on their state's exit exam in mathematics the first time they took the exam. Those figures represent data from only 18 states. (See table 6.2.)

SEAs do not calculate formally the number of students potentially affected by CSEM. Tienken (2011) calculated or estimated the numbers from available SEA data. Although the calculations of students potentially affected by CSEM are tentative, they represent the best estimate possible given the lack of data provided by SEAs on this subject.

The fact remains that students are being miscategorized and subjected to inappropriate education decisions that carry high stakes for them and their families based on either an inability or unwillingness of SEAs to

Table 6.2.   State CSEM in Scale-Score Points for the LA and Mathematics Sections of High School Exit Exams (n = 23) and Number of Testing Opportunities

State/Year	LA CSEM	Mathematics CSEM	Testing Opportunities
Alabama	Did not respond	Did not respond	Not available
Alaska 2007	19	19	3
Arizona 2007	13	8	3
California 2007	11	9	8
Florida 2005	15	13	3
Georgia 2007	6	6	3
Idaho 2007	3.15	3.24	3
Indiana 2006	Did not respond	Did not respond	3
Louisiana 2006	3.54	3.98	3
Massachusetts 2007	Not reported	Not reported	3
Minnesota 2007	14	12	3
Missouri 2007	Approx. 8	Approx. 9	> 1
Nevada 2007	26	33	> 3
New Jersey 2006	Not reported	Not reported	3
New Mexico 2006	10	7	2
New York 2006	Not reported	Not reported	2
North Carolina	Not available	Not available	3
Ohio 2006	Approx. 8.59	Approx. 10.02	5
South Carolina 2004	5.6	5.5	3
Tennessee 2007	Not available	Not available	3
Texas 2007	Not available	Not available	3
Virginia 2004	24	17	Not available
Washington 2007	8.99	8.44	3

Adapted from: Tienken, C. H. (2011). High School Exit Exams and Mismeasurement. *The Educational Forum,* 4(75): 298–314.

address this issue. SEAs are welcome and encouraged to respond with more exact figures to bring transparency and clarity to this topic (Tienken, 2011).

HOW MUCH MONEY DOES YOUR MOM MAKE?

As introduced in a previous chapter, money matters when it comes to achievement on standardized tests. Therefore, CSEM is even more pressing for students labeled as economically disadvantaged. A review of test-score data collected by the Center for Education Progress revealed that students labeled as economically disadvantaged, as a group, always score lower on all statewide exams, including high school exit exams, than their non–economically disadvantaged peers.

The average effect size difference is greater than 0.50. Table 6.3 includes examples of effect size differences from several states' high school exams between students labeled as economically disadvantaged or eligible for free or reduced lunch and more advantaged students.

The range of effect sizes in table 6.3 is 0.57 to 1.05, meaning if the average score of the non–economically disadvantaged group scored at the 50th percentile, the group labeled as economically disadvantaged would score between the 30th and 14th percentiles given the range of effect sizes in table 6.3. The effect size differences remain relatively consistent for statewide tests given in grades 3 through 11 (Tienken, 2011).

Tienken (2008b) reported an example of how economics impact test scores from an entire testing program in his review of the New Jersey

Table 6.3. Mean Scale Scores and Effect Size differences on Statewide High School Exams in Mathematics (M) and Reading/Language Arts (LA) for Students Labeled Economically Disadvantaged and Not Disadvantaged

State		Economically Disadvantaged	Not Disadvantaged	Effect Size
CA	(LA)	365.91	389.78	0.69
	(M)	370.68	391.55	0.57
CT	(LA)	211.40	254.50	1.05
	(M)	218.20	264.30	1.02
DE	(LA)	501.82	525.17	0.67
	(M)	518.66	542.52	0.77
IL	(LA)	148.39	159.69	0.81
	(M)	147.62	160.60	0.94
PA	(LA)	1220	1410	0.75
	(M)	1210	1390	0.74
TX	(LA)	2217	2296	0.60
	(M)	2115	2217	0.59

Source: Tienken, C. H. (2010, Fall). Social Inequity and High School Test Scores: More Strong Correlations. *AASA Journal of Scholarship and Practice,* 7(3): 3–5.

state testing program in grades 3 and 8. The New Jersey Department of Education (NJDOE) reports statewide test results in several forms, including by district factor group (DFG). The DFG rankings are a rough approximation of a community's overall wealth. New Jersey SEAs categorize districts on a continuum of A through J, with A districts located in the state's poorest communities and J districts located in the state's wealthiest communities.

The education bureaucrats at the NJDOE, some policy makers, and some education leaders use DFG as a proxy for the socioeconomic status (SES) of students. The descriptive data for New Jersey test results (see table 6.4) provided by the NJDOE produced a Spearman's Rho correlation coefficient of 1.0 (p ≤ . 001). In essence, the New Jersey tests tell more about how much a child's "mom makes" than about the quality of the education he/she receives or how hard that child works in school.

The DFG data demonstrate a perfect, positive relationship between being economically disadvantaged and performance on the state assessments, identical to what Nairn (1980) observed with the SAT data discussed in a previous chapter. NJDOE personnel conduct regular meetings to determine whether the items offend or reflect bias against any minority group.

The majority of the A districts, the state's poorest districts, are located in urban areas, and the majority of New Jersey's poorest minority students live in urban districts. As can be seen from table 6.4, the aggregate

Table 6.4. Percentage of General Education Students in Each DFG Who Scored Proficient or Advanced Proficient on the LA and Mathematics Sections of the NJ ASK 3, 4 & GEPA (NJDOE, 2006; 2006a)

DFG	LA			Mathematics		
	3rd	4th	8th	3rd	4th	8th
A	66.2	74.2	55.9	57.8	59.6	40.1
B	81.1	85.6	75.2	75.2	70.6	60.7
CD	83.9	89.4	79.2	80.4	75.3	65.9
DE	90.3	93.4	84.7	85.9	80.7	72.4
FG	91.8	94.6	88.1	86.9	82.6	78.6
GH	93.3	95.5	91.5	90.1	85.4	82.9
I	96.5	97.9	95	93.6	90.5	88.2
J	96.8	98.6	97.2	93.8	91.7	94.6
Spearman Rho (r_s)	1.0[a]	1.0[a]	1.0[a]	1.0[a]	1.0[a]	1.0[a]

Source: Public Domain
[a]Statistically significant at p ≤ .01

student populations who attend districts in the factor groups closest to district factor group A without fail, always score lower than those closest to group J.

The Color of Money

In general, the relationship between money and test scores exists nationally on all state tests currently given. According to an analysis of state test results data found on the Center on Education Policy website (www. cep-dc.org), at no grade level on any state test does the group of students labeled economically disadvantaged exhibit a higher mean score than the group of students labeled as non–economically disadvantaged.

Remember that we discussed that one aim of the dual system of education is to provide benefits, through a higher-quality education, to the "haves" and relegate the "have-nots" to a more mechanistic, lower-quality education. In this country, in many instances, this relationship between quality education and less quality plays out in color; that is, the color of children's skin.

The percentage of African Americans living at or below the poverty line was 24.1 percent, almost one in four, in 2003, and 21.8 percent of Hispanics lived at or below the poverty line. Only 12.5 percent of Whites lived at or below the poverty line in 2003 (U.S. Department of Health and Human Services, 2004). By 2008, the percentage of Whites living at or below the poverty line dropped to 8.6 percent, whereas the percentage increased to 24.7 percent for African Americans and 23.2 percent for Hispanics (U.S. Census Bureau, 2009).

The statistics are not better for children. According to the U.S. Census Bureau (2009), 33.9 percent of African American children live at or below the poverty line, 30.6 percent of Hispanic children, and 10.6 percent of White children. Because wealth plays such a large part in achievement on standardized tests, at least 0.50 effect size on average, it is easy to see how CSEM, poverty, and intellectually vapid reform policies work to create the perfect storm of potential negative consequences for children of poverty, a disproportionate amount of whom are children of color.

STANDARDS FOR REPORTING

Not all SEAs adhere to the standards, best practices, and recommendations regarding CSEM advocated in the *Standards for Educational and Psychological Testing* (AERA, APA & NCME, 1999). For example, Standard 2.2 (AERA, APA & NCME, 1999) reads, "The standard error of measurement, both overall and conditional . . . , should be reported . . . in units of each derived score" (p. 31). Tienken (2011) found that almost 25 percent of the states did not report CSEM data for their test results.

When SEA personnel choose not to report the CSEM (Standard 2.2), it creates a snowball effect of *Standards* violations. "When test score information is released to parents . . . , those responsible for the testing programs should provide appropriate interpretations. The interpretations should describe in simple language . . . the precision of the scores and common misinterpretations of test scores . . ." (AERA, APA & NCME, 1999: Standard 5.10, p. 65). "When relevant for test interpretation, test documents ordinarily should include item level information, cut-scores . . . the standard errors of measurement" (AERA, APA & NCME, 1999: Standard 6.5, p. 69).

School administrators, students, and parents in states where SEAs do not report CSEM or do not publish technical manuals in the public domain have no mechanism by which to judge the precision of individual student test results. Thus, stakeholders are limited in attempts to appeal the results or lobby for changes to the system (Tienken & Rodriguez, 2010). How can school administrators initiate policy remedies or safeguards for problems that they do not know exist? Where is the institutional accountability, and where are procedural safety valves for children?

Is CSEM a real concern for students? Yes, according to the leadership of APA, AERA, NCME, and JCTP and individuals in the field of educational testing like Messick (1996) and Koretz (2008), because even a small amount of CSEM can have severe consequences for students when SEA personnel do not account for it and instead simply require students to achieve a set cut score to demonstrate proficiency (Koretz, 2008) as do all states.

Because high school exit exams and standardized state exams in grades 3 through 8 are used nationwide, and will be for the foreseeable future, CSEM is a major issue that is not being addressed. We can be sure that perhaps hundreds of thousands of youth might have been potentially affected negatively in the NCLB era by what we perceive as inaction at the state and national levels to develop policy remedies aligned with standards and recommendations for appropriate testing practices.

Conclusions about State-Mandated Exams

Tienken (2011) found that almost all of the states with high school exit exams provided a basic policy remedy to try to account for CSEM: multiple testing opportunities. Although this seems like a positive approach, it does not overcome the issue and simply shifts the CSEM to another test (Koretz, 2008) and does not account for it in the interpretation phase.

It is important to keep in mind that many countries around the world engage in standardized testing to sort students into academic and vocational tracks, gatekeep some students from accessing the total curriculum, and overtly manage their country's current social-class structures and human capital. Sorting students in Europe via standardized testing is a left-over cultural practice from the days of the aristocracies and restrictive class systems. The practice of sorting and gatekeeping is generally accepted culturally in other parts of the world like in some Asian countries, but it is not necessarily part of the democratic culture and ideals in the United States.

Those who hold a democratic, Jeffersonian view of education reject sorting systems, whether those systems are overt or covert. After all, the public school system in the United States is the only social institution that allows democratic values to be passed on to the next generation, and it is the only institution with the ability to socialize all Americans, citizens and immigrants alike, to the democratic ideas of the country (Commission on the Reorganization of Secondary Education, 1918).

The larger policy question remains: Given what we know about the effect of CSEM on score interpretation and the high-stakes negative social and educational consequences to youth associated with score imprecision, do the ends (e.g., the mythical standardizing of the high school diploma) justify the means of using high-stakes tests with known technical flaws that affect score interpretation? Children do not have a seat at the decision-making table. Policy must speak for them. Adults make policy.

TRUE CONFESSIONS FROM A HIGH-STAKES SCORER

One brave soul, John Koudela III (2005, February), provided some very revealing insights into the scoring procedures used in the standard test industry. He submitted a report to Marda Kirkwood of Citizens United for Responsible Education (CURE, February 2005), the essence of which we report here with Mr. Koudela's permission.

At the time, Mr. Koudela held a BS degree and had been employed in the electronics manufacturing industry until he, like millions across America, was laid off from his job because of the cost-cutting functions of companies during the recession that started in 2001. He applied to a NCS Pearson Performance Scoring Center in 2003, while still continuing to seek work in his own field, and was hired to correct state high-stakes tests.

Allegedly, Pearson hired approximately 350 college-degreed individuals as their temporary employee pool to grade state high-stakes tests at $11.40 per hour. The work was full time, five days a week, without benefits or days off. After two days of training, the fun began. Koudela observed that scorers had discovered some test answers that were questionable, but that fact could not be discussed. Test scorers were told to accept only those answers approved by the "Range Finding Committee" regardless of their own college-educated knowledge base.

However, scoring criteria did change as scorers came up with more student test answers that were found to be acceptable, but were not in the original rubrics. Those new answers were approved by supervisors "on the spot," as was apparently allowed, although scorers were told that they were not to worry about re-scoring previous tests that might also contain those correct answers.

One day's "correct" answers for a given question would be suddenly changed, and answers that had been wrong were suddenly correct! Whatever rubrics or criteria for grading were changed, it was of no concern to scorers; just meet the work quota as accurately as you can with the approved answers. Scorers were constantly reminded about how many tests they needed to finish each day and how many days were left to score the remaining tests.

Each day scorers were pushed by supervisors to read more tests. There were very few scorers who had both a high number of reads and high reliability percentages. Over 38 different criteria were ultimately listed for just one open-ended science question alone. At the end of scoring a test, scorers were ordered to destroy all their notes they collected to assist them in scoring test answers.

Mr. Koudela closed his report stating: "Conformance was the main issue, not students' ability to logically arrive at their answers or rely on their own experience! This was true of all test scoring of all test answers." Test scorers were reminded daily to remember that "The chair is orange, if the 'committee' says so."

Not an Isolated Case

Providing more data and additional credibility to Mr. Koudela's report is the August 27, 2000, headline, by reporter Jolayne Houtz of the *Seattle Times*, that "Temps spend just minutes to score state test; A WASL math problem may take 20 seconds and essay, 2-1/2 minutes." The reporter visited the Iowa City NCS test-scoring facility (NCS was purchased by Pearson PLC of the United Kingdom for $2.5 billion).

Houtz reported that the scorers work at "assembly-line pace" and read as many as 180 writing essays a day with an average of 2 1/2 minutes per essay. Houtz noted that nine of ten WASL exams were graded by a single reader, and even if a second reader scored the exam, the first reader's score counted. In the year 2000, NCS expected to hand-score 82 million student responses. She quoted one NCS scorer as saying that when the pressure built to meet deadlines, supervisors announced, "Don't pay as much attention to accuracy." Houtz was never asked to withdraw her reported statements.

Writing in the September 14, 2005, issue of the *Spokesman-Review* of Spokane, Washington, Linda Bauer stated that as a scorer of the fourth-grade WASL writing examinations during the summer of 2005, she had received two nine-hour days of training by Pearson Measurement, the contractor for the WASL. She was then assigned 500 student essays to correct, and she noted that she was never certain how to score them.

Bauer wrote that the WASL anchor papers (the models to follow) simply confused the scorers. This certainly substantiates the Koudela and Houtz statements. Bauer concluded that the result of the writing exam given to students, parents, and teachers "doesn't tell anyone what needs to be learned" (p. B-5). Only a number is reported, a 1 or 2 means fail, and a 3 or 4 means pass—so much for the touted WASL feedback.

In December 2005, newspapers across the country reported that a testing company in Ohio had failed to grade state-mandated tests correctly. Measurement, Inc., graded 1,599 Ohio high-stakes graduation tests and failed 890 students. Apparently a conversion of raw test data was the source of the errors. Oh, only 272 school districts were affected. How many more test errors does the state of Ohio, or any other state for that matter, need to see an "unsolvable problem"? Is this education reform?

POINTS TO REMEMBER

A *social contract* has long been made where organized societies and governments initiate interrelationships that support its citizenry. This social contract has been made to support public education by virtue of the 10th Amendment to the U.S. Constitution and the respective state constitutions. This unwritten contract endorses a positive support-base for all school-age youth. The NCLB Act subversively negated this contract by terminating the word "social" and substituting the word "corporate."

The *corporate contract* means that the schools are no longer social institutions with the primary mission of serving and educating youth. Current policy endorses a corporate-profit model instead. Millions of youth will fall into the "social junkyard" because they did not perform mechanistically, like a programmed machine, on one high-stakes test. *Corporation USA* has no need for losers.

A LOOK AHEAD

Chapter 7 explores the Common Core State Standards initiative and provides evidence to suggest the project is misguided. Perhaps the most astonishing thing to us about the standards project is that there is no empirical evidence to support it. We will argue forcefully that standardization and homogenization of children is not only morally bankrupt, but empirically vapid as well.

NOTE

The writers thank the *Clearing House* journal for permission to use excerpts in this chapter from Orlich's "The No Child Left Behind Act: An Illogical Accountability Model" 78(1): 6–11, September/October 2004. The writers thank Dr. David C. Berliner for his insights leading to the section on the social contract.

REFERENCES

American Educational Research Association, American Psychological Association & National Council on Measurement in Education (1999). *Standards for educational and psychological testing*, Washington, DC: American Educational Research Association.

Amrein, A. L. & Berliner, D. C. (2002a). High-Stakes Testing, Uncertainty and Student Learning. *Educational Policy Analysis Archives* 10(18): 1–56, March 28. Review at epaa.asu.edu/epaa/v10n18.

Amrein, A. L. & Berliner, D. C. (2002b). An Analysis of Some Unintended and Negative Consequences of High-Stakes Testing. Education Policy Research Unit, Education Policy Studies Laboratory, Arizona State University, Tempe, A, December (EPSL0211125-EPRU).

Bauer, L. (2005). "WASL Too Nebulous." Spokane, WA: *The Spokesman-Review*, p. B-5.

Booher-Jennings, J. (2005). Below the Bubble: "Educational Triage" and the Texas Accountability System. *American Educational Research Journal*, 42(2), 231–268.

Borg, M., Plumlee, P. & Stranahan, H. (2007). Plenty of Children Left Behind: High-Stakes Testing and Graduation Rates in Duval County, Florida. Educational Policy 2: 695–716.

Braun, H. (2004). Reconsidering the Impact of High-Stakes Testing. *Education Policy Analysis Archives* 12(1): January 5. Review at epaa.asu.edu/epaa/v12n1.

Burch, P. (2005). The new educational privatization: Educational contracting and high-stakes accountability. *Teachers College Record* (online). Retrieved October 2, 2009, from www.tcrecord.org/content.asp?contentid=12259.

Cohen, J. (1988). *Statistical Power Analysis for the Behavioral Sciences*, 2nd ed. Hillsdale, NH: Lawrence Erlbaum Associates.

Commission on the Reorganization of Secondary Education. (1918). *Cardinal Principles of Secondary Education*. Washington, DC: U.S. Bureau of Education, Bulletin No. 35.

Council of Chief State School Officers. (2009). *Common core state standards initiative: Frequently asked questions*. Author. Retrieved October 8, 2009, from www.corestandards.org/.

Darling-Hammond, L. (2003). Standards and Assessments: Where We Are and What We Need. *Teachers College Record*. Review at:www.tcrecord.org/Contentasp?ContentID=11109.

Education Commission of the States. (2008). *State Notes: Exit Exams*. Denver, CO: Author. Available at mb2.ecs.org/reports/Report.aspx?id=1357.

Gayler, K., Chudowsky, N., Kober, N. & Hamilton, M. (2003). *State High School Exit Exams Put to the Test*. Washington, DC: Center on Education Policy.

Haney, W. (2002, May 6). Lake Woebeguaranteed: Misuse of Test Scores in Massachusetts, Part I. *The Education Policy Analysis Archives* 10(24). Review at epaa.asu.edu/epaa/v10n24.

Harville, L. M. (1991). Standard Error of Measurement. *Educational Measurement: Issues and Practices* 10(2): 33–41.

Houtz, J. (2000, August 27). Temps Spend Just Minutes to Score State Test: A WASL Math Problem May Take 20 Seconds; An Essay, 2-1/2 Minutes. Seattle: *Seattle Times*.

Koretz, D. (2008). *Measuring Up: What Educational Testing Really Tells Us*. Cambridge, MA: Harvard University Press.

Koudela, J. III. (2005, February). "On Scoring of OPT/WASL Educational Assessments." Report submitted to Marda Kirkwood, Citizens United for Responsible Education, Burien, Washington. (Reported with permission.)

Levin, H. M. (2009). The Economic Payoff to Investing in Educational Justice. *Educational Researcher* 38(1): 5–20.

Linn, R. L. & Haug, C. (2002). Stability of School-Building Accountability Scores and Gains. *Educational Evaluation and Policy Analysis* 24(1), 29–36.

Messick, S. (1996). *Validity of Performance Assessments.* In *Technical Issues in Large-Scale Performance Assessment.* G. W. Phillips (Ed.), 1–18. Washington, DC: National Center for Educational Statistics.

Nairn, A. (Ed.). (1980). *The Reign of ETS: The Corporation That Makes Up Minds.* Washington, DC: Ralph Nader Report.

No Child Left Behind (NCLB) Act of 2001, Pub. L. No. 107-110, § 115, Stat. 1425 (2002).

Orlich, D. C. (2003). An Examination of the Longitudinal Effect of the Washington Assessment of Student Learning (WASL) on Student Achievement. *Education Policy Analysis Archives* 11(18). Review at:epaa.asu.edu/epaa/v11n18.

Sanger, David. (1978). "Is 'Competency' Good Enough?" *New York Times,* April 2, p. WC3. Available: ProQuest—Historical New York Times.

Tienken, C. H. (2011). Structured Inequity: The Intersection of Socioeconomic Status and the Standard Error of Measurement of State Mandated High School Test Results. NCPEA Yearbook, 257–271.

Tienken, C. H. (2008a). A Descriptive Study of the Technical Characteristics of the Results of New Jersey's Assessments of Skills and Knowledge in Grades 3, 4, and GEPA. *New Jersey Journal of Supervision and Curriculum Development* 52: 46–61.

Tienken, C. H. (2008b). The Characteristics of State Assessment Results. *Academic Exchange Quarterly* 12(3): 34–39.

Tienken, C. H. & Rodriguez, O. (2010). The Error of State-Mandated High School Exams. *Academic Exchange Quarterly* 14(2): 50–55.

United States Census Bureau. (2009). Income, poverty and health insurance coverage in the United States: 2008. Author. Retrieved from:www.census.gov/Press-Release/www/releases/archives/income_wealth/014227.html.

United States Department of Health and Human Services. (2004). Indicators of welfare dependence: Annual report to Congress 2004. Washington, DC: Author.

Wallis, C. (8 June, 2008). No Child Left Behind: Doomed to Fail. *Time* magazine.

Wilson, R. J. (1999). Aspects of Validity in Large-Scale Programs of Student Assessment. *Alberta Journal of Educational Research* 45(4): Winter, 333–343.

SEVEN

World-Class Standards That Are Too Big to Fail

Education reform in the United States is being driven largely by ideology, intuition, and dogma—oops, we meant to write "World-Class Standards." The newest installment of standards represents just another attempt to homogenize schooling. The ideas put forth today are no different from those presented by the Committee of 10 and Committee of 15 in 1893 and 1895. As we demonstrated in the first part of the book, the drive to standardize education for some, usually the less fortunate of society, has been going on for some time.

ENTER THE COMMON CORE STATE STANDARDS INITIATIVE

In March 2010, governors and education bureaucrats from 48 states, plus two territories and the District of Columbia, endorsed developing and implementing a common core of state standards for selected content areas for grades K-12. The CCSS just happens to be supported by Achieve, Business Roundtable, U.S. Chamber of Commerce, the U.S. Army, and a host of other organizations. The general criteria used to develop the CCSS are listed below:

- Alignment with college and work expectations;
- Inclusion of rigorous content *and* application of knowledge through high-order skills;
- Built upon strengths and lessons of current state standards;
- Informed by top-performing countries, so that all students are prepared to succeed in our global economy and society;
- Evidence and/or research based.

Translating CCSSI Standards-Setting

According to the writers of the CCSS, seven major considerations guided their development. Below is a brief description of that set. Keep in mind that the standards development really means that the vendors of the CCSS will proclaim that all high school students will be college prepared based on one set of curriculum standards for the third most populated country on the planet. The vendors trumpet "fewer, clearer, higher" from upon high.

One purported goal of the CCSS process was to produce a set of fewer, clearer, and higher standards so that any standard could be translatable to and teachable in the classroom. However, when one actually dissects the standards into the specific learning objectives that will be necessary for teachers to teach, one will see quickly that there are not fewer, clearer standards at all.

Evidence?

The writers of the CCSS stated they "made unprecedented use of evidence" in deciding what to include—or not include—in the standards. We cannot let this consideration skip by without noting that in NO case was there any field or pilot testing of any standard in a classroom. What the writers call evidence and research simply comes down to opinions of individuals or organizations with all being footnoted.

Absolutely NO experimental or control groups were used to evaluate the quality or efficacy of the standards! Empirical methods were not used to determine the efficacy of these standards. There is no independently verified empirical evidence supporting this initiative. This point is most critical, because once again we see a batch of brief enthusiasms and ideological advocacy labeled as research!

Does monitorial instruction ring a bell? Think back to the first part of this book when that "great idea" was introduced as a way to make urban education more efficient. Efficiency is not necessarily effective. Below we take some of the claims made by the vendors of the CCSS and provide translations of the considerations they made when constructing the standards.

Internationally benchmarked: The vendors claim that these standards are mirrors of standards of high-performing countries and states so that all students are prepared to succeed in a global economy and society. Translation: We copied some language from some of the best test-taking nations, but we have no evidence that ideas we copied will have any positive influence on student learning in the United States and we have not considered any unintended consequences.

Special populations: The standards are written with inclusionary language, or so the vendors tell us. Translation: The authors of the CCSS assume that the standards are accessible to different learners, but because the CCSS were never field tested prior to launch, the vendors do not have data to support the assertion.

Assessment: We are told that the authors of the CCSS did not develop an assessment system. Translation: The vendors do state that these standards will ultimately be the basis for an assessment system that would be a "national" assessment to monitor implementation. Now that most states agreed on the final standards, testing is scheduled to begin in 2014 or 2015, depending on the state. In many states the results from the national tests will be used to gauge the quality of the public system and those who work in it. All of the NCLB waiver plans approved by the USDOE included the use of the CCSS and national assessment tied to incentives (aka consequence) for teachers and school administrators.

Standards and curriculum: The vendors of the CCSS correctly note that the standards are not a set of curricula. They state that this initiative is about developing a set of standards that are common across states. They claim that any specific curriculum that follows will continue to be a local responsibility (or state-led, where appropriate): They claim the illusion of local control.

Translation: However, it will be the national test frameworks and eventually released items that become the actual local curriculum. That is because of the austere stakes attached to the results of the national test. For example, as soon as it is determined that algebra makes up over 60 percent of the national mathematics exam and geometry accounts for, let's say, 22 percent, you will see a massive shift in local curriculum away from geometry and more time toward algebra.

Twenty-first-century skills: The CCSS focused on two areas—English-language arts and mathematics. The vendors claim that the standards have incorporated twenty-first-century skills where possible. Translation: We think twenty-first-century skills consist of a narrow conception of mathematics and western English language arts. We have no idea how to develop authentic twenty-first-century skills such (1) strategizing, (2) entrepreneurship, (3) persistence, (4) empathy, (5) socially conscious problem solving, (6) cross-cultural collaboration and cooperation, (7) intellectual and social curiosity, (8) drive, (9) risk taking, and (10) challenging the status quo, and our austere testing program will only work to narrow and reduce the curriculum to what is tested.

The vendors of the CCSS claim college readiness is a key twenty-first-century skill. We do refer you to the May 14, 2010, Associated Press news release by Alan Scher Zagier, who reported that the need for a four-year college diploma is being challenged by economists and policy analysts. Other economists were quoted as finding the number of new jobs requiring a college degree is less than the actual number of college graduates.

We suggest our readers visit the U.S. Bureau of Labor Statistics page, especially the Employment Projections sections of the site, and look at the ten-year labor projections. Most of the top-20 largest-employing job fields and the fastest-growing job fields do not require a B.A. degree. So, again we caution *Caveat Emptor!*

Frankly Speaking

Let us be very frank: the CCSS are no improvement over the plethora of state standards that now abound in the Unites States. The CCSS are simply another set of lists of performance objectives. Ohanian (1999) warned about this type of project years ago. The CCSS vendors tend to assume that customized curriculum will be developed either by the respective states or textbook companies.

In fact, most large publishers had new texts on the market soon after the CCSS were released. So much for customization. It was like the publishers had the books on the shelves ready to go before the standards were even released. Did they drive this effort? That is amazing to us. These standards were supposed to be drastically different from what existed, yet in a matter of weeks new "Common Core" materials were available for purchase.

Some state boards of education, like New Jersey, actually mandated school district use of the Common Core less than a year after they were released. This meant that almost 600 school districts in the state began to purchase brand-new texts with millions of taxpayer dollars. It did not matter if the school district personnel had just revised their math curricula and purchased new texts two years earlier. All that was now obsolete. Let's call this what it is: a subsidy for text and test publishers. The CCSS does not have anything to do with education. It has to do everything with the business of education.

CHALLENGING THE CCSS

After we began work on this book, in came an empirical challenge to the Common Core State Standards. On July 21, 2010, William J. Mathis published a policy brief titled *The "Common Core" Standards Initiative: An Effective Reform Tool?* Below is an excerpt from the Executive Summary.

> The Obama administration advocates for education standards designed to make all high school graduates—college- and career-ready. To achieve this end, the administration is exerting pressure on states to adopt content standards, known as the common core. . . . Contentions about global competitiveness provide a key rationale given for common standards, along with increasing equity and streamlining the reform process. . . .
>
> U.S. states with high academic standards fare no better (or worse) than those identified as having low academic standards. Research support for standards-driven, test-based accountability systems is similar-

ly weak. And nations with centralized standards generally tend to per-form no better (or worse) on inter-national tests than those without.

The NGA/CCSSO standards-development process was completed quickly—in approximately one year—by Achieve, Inc., a private contractor. This brief raises several concerns about the development, content, and use of those 500 pages of standards and supporting documents. For instance, the level of input from school-based practitioners appears to be minimal, the standards themselves have not been field tested, and it is unclear whether the tests used to measure the academic out-comes of common standards will have sufficient validity to justify the high-stakes consequences that will likely arise around their use. Accordingly, it seems improbable that the common core standards will have the positive effects on educational quality or equality being sought by proponents, particularly in light of the lack of essential capacity at the local, state and federal levels.

Common Core Standards: Where's That Evidence?

We have seen many negative consequences of state-mandated curriculum and assessment schemes in terms of curricular reductionism. Study after study reports the elimination of the arts and physical education, the overteaching of mathematics and language arts to the detriment of science, social studies, foreign language, and other "non-core areas, and the over reliance of high stakes commercially prepared state tests to monitor the implementation of standards" (Au, 2007; Booher-Jennings, 2005).

The CCSS will exacerbate the current high-stakes testing environment. Although the CCSS are marketed as something to provide greater instructional guidance, the probability is likely that high-stakes testing will be used to enforce implementation of the CCSS.

The Council of Chief State School Officers (CCSSO, 2009), one of the organizations that pushed through the development of the standards, wrote, "States know that standards alone cannot propel the systems change we need. The common core state standards will enable participating states to . . . develop and implement an assessment system to measure student performance against the common core state standards" (p. 2).

These standards will form the core curriculum of every public school program, drive another stronger wave of high-stakes testing, and thus become student selection criteria for K-12 school programs such as Title I services, gifted and talented programs, high school course placement, and other academic programs.

Campbell's Law (Campbell, 1976) predicts what will happen: the subjects prescribed currently by the CCSS, language arts and mathematics, and eventually science, will become the most important subjects in terms of time and resources allotted to teachers. The opportunities students have to explore and delve into other subjects and educational activities, especially those seen as not academic enough, will atrophy further.

Eventually, within three to five years of having the CCSS and the accompanying high-stakes national test, we will see students who do not meet the arbitrary levels of achievement set in those subject areas be labeled "at risk" and forced to do more work in those areas, depriving them further of the opportunities to participate in other educational activities.

We cite three to five years because that was the approximate time frame when schools across the country began to act regressively because of the NCLB curriculum and testing mandates. Perhaps, because the regressive infrastructure is already in place, it will happen faster. We know for sure based on the Race to the Top (RTTT) competition and the ESEA blueprint for reauthorization that teachers in schools whose students do well in those areas will be rewarded.

Teachers in schools in which students do less well will be punished, leading to a nation of schools that focus only on two or three subject areas. It's already happening in the RTTT states and even in states like Colorado that passed legislation allowing such non-evidence-based practices in hopes of getting a RTTT grant.

Life, Liberty, and the Pursuit of Standardization

We need to examine the underlying theories and applied research that demonstrate standards can help us achieve our goals for education. The notion that a human being can be standardized rests upon theories of behaviorism and efficiency. Both have served education poorly, but for some reason retain their attractiveness with policy makers and some educators. As Callahan (1962) so thoroughly exposed, education leaders supported Frederick Taylor's Scientific Management (1947) and tried to make education more efficient like business. Whether business was more efficient or more effective for children was never really questioned.

Remember, efficiency is not the same as effectiveness, and effectiveness is not always efficient. Efficiency is concerned with maximizing profit at all costs, as we have painfully witnessed and experienced as a result of the hyper profit-efficiency movement currently running Wall Street. Also remember that Taylor's ideas of efficiency and scientific management were created in the steel mills focused on the shoveling of coal, an inanimate object.

School leaders work with children, human beings. There is no evidence that the efficiency movement of the late 1800s and early 1900s improved education; in fact evidence exists that the opposite was true. Consider that the public high school graduation rate in 1918, well into the efficiency movement, was about 4 percent.

When we think of standardized instruction, the idea of programmed or scripted instruction comes to mind. We are not sure if that is what is best for students, because not all students learn at the same speeds; develop cognitively, socially, or morally at the same rates; or react to instruction the same ways. Standardized instruction assumes all those variables are stable with all students at all times. However, students bring various levels of prior experience, emotions, and attitudes to the classroom.

Standardized Instruction

Standardized instruction deskills teaching and reduces it to a recipe and a set of steps. The problem is that students do not always act or respond according to what the teacher's manual says. If we deskill the job of teaching even further than it has already become through the various whole school reform models and canned programs, then teachers will not know how to problem solve instructional issues that do not conform to what the teacher's manual prescribes. They will not be able to individualize instruction or meet the needs of diverse learners.

Those of you who spend time in classrooms know the difference between someone who can teach and someone who is simply following the teaching manual. Teachers solve instructional problems; automatons that read teacher's manuals and follow scripted programs cause instructional problems for others to solve. Teachers who are forced to follow programmed or scripted programs do not create learning, they imitate learning and they pass that penchant for imitation on to their students, thereby deskilling their students along with themselves.

Curricular Distance

Once again, everyone should ask what are the underlying theories and applied research that demonstrate one set of national standards will raise student achievement for a diverse group of students? One problem with standards developed at the national level is that the curriculum becomes further removed from the people who actually have to use it: teachers, students, and administrators.

Curriculum organization and articulation is what some have called a proximal variable (Wang, Haertel & Walberg, 1993). That means it becomes most influential when it is closer to the student. Curriculum must be designed and developed locally, by the teachers, administrators, and students who use and experience it, to have the greatest influence (Tanner & Tanner, 2007; Tramaglini, 2010; Wang, Haertel & Walberg, 1993).

The influence of curriculum on student achievement lessens the more distal curriculum becomes from the end users. The design and organization of the curriculum at the local level were two of the strongest administratively mutable variables identified by Wang, Haertel, and Walberg (1993) that affected student achievement. State governance and policy setting was the weakest variable. We wonder about the influence of national governance in what used to be a locally controlled system.

We note for the reader the lack of evidence that mandating the same standards for all students improves achievement. The opposite is true. One set of curriculum standards will exacerbate learning problems for students whose cognitive developmental stage does not match the curriculum expectations (Orlich, 2007; Piaget, 1983; Sweller, 2006).

SOME RECENT EVIDENCE AGAINST STANDARDIZATION FOR ALL

The slowing of growth on NAEP is a canary in the coal mine. Proponents of the CCSS say they will raise student achievement and help close the achievement gap—among other things. Unfortunately for proponents of national standards, the recent evidence does not bode well for that logic chain.

Consider that many states did not have mandatory curriculum standards or testing in most grade levels prior 2002. Records from the Council of Chief State School Officers indicated that only 21 states had standards in at least mathematics and language arts by 1999 and fewer had standards in science. So prior to NCLB less than 50 percent of the states had mandatory standards and tests in mathematics and language arts.

The report released by the National Center for Educational Statistics on April 28, 2009, of the recent NAEP reading results provided some examples of what a focus on standards can produce. A review of the age 9 reading scores shows a slowdown in academic achievement as measured by NAEP.

We chose age 9 because those are the students most likely to show achievement influences from NCLB because they were in school since the inception of the law in 2002. To be fair, we will not look at the scores from 2002 until now. We present the scores from 2004 to 2008 because that provides schools two years to implement the law (2002–2004) and then four years until the NAEP testing date in 2008.

Theoretically, the reading scores from the 9-year-olds should be the strongest of any age group. They entered school two years after the law was enacted and experienced it at its height. We will compare those scores to the 1999–2004 scores, the time when fewer states had mandatory standards and tests in reading. During the 1999–2004 time period reading scores for all students rose seven points but rose only four points for the 2004–2008 time period. That statistic could be misleading because of Simpson's Paradox. A more honest comparison is that of specific ethnic groups.

The gap between students identified as Black and those identified as White narrowed by three points during the NCLB era, but it narrowed nine points during the previous period. The gap closed three times as much prior to NCLB. The gap between students identified as Hispanic and Whites closed almost twice as much prior to NCLB than after; seven points closure prior and four points after.

Some might point to that and say, "yes," that proves that the states lowered their standards during NCLB. However, remember that less than 50 percent of the states had mandatory standards prior to the NCLB era. Some might still say that is why we need new national standards to keep state education bureaucrats honest. Once again, the NAEP scores were better before all states had standards and even now, many states' standards are strikingly similar in mathematics and language arts. You can go to nationsreportcard.gov/ltt_2008/ to review the NAEP results and trends. Yes, we know. There is one more argument to slay.

Not True

There does not exist a strong correlation and certainly not a cause-and-effect relationship between national standards and national performance. There is empirical evidence, easily locatable, to debunk that fallacy. Studies from the last 11 years show that the relationship between rankings on international tests and the economic vitality of the top 17 economies in the world are either negative or so weak that they are not significant, and certainly do not demonstrate a cause-and-effect relationship (Baker; 2010; Bracey, 2005; Krueger, 1999; Psacharopoulos & Patrinos, 2002; Ramirez, Luo, Schofer & Meyer, 2006).

The strongest 17 economies in the world actually show a negative relationship between their ranking on international tests and economic strength (Tienken, 2008). With the data so prevalent to the contrary, why do proponents continue to use the economic competeriveness argument? Is this a case of anti-intellectualism driving policy?

There are more countries in the world that have national standards, so as a matter of probability, there can be more countries with national standards that scored well. Second, looking at the test results, we can see that some countries that outrank us on international tests have national standards and some do not. For example, in the 2006 PIRLS study of reading achievement (see timss.bc.edu/PDF/P06_IR_Ch1.pdf), Canada did very well, but it does not have national standards.

The same can be said of the international PISA test results. The 2006 science PISA results show Canada and Australia perform well above the OECD average, ranking #2 and #4 among OECD countries respectively (OECD, 2007). Canada and Australia do not have national standards. They had similar rankings on the 2003 PISA results, with Canada ranking #4 and Australia #7 in math, both #4 in problem solving, and Canada #2 and Australia #3 in reading.

There are plenty of countries with national curriculum and standards that perform much worse than these two countries and the United States

(OECD, 2003). Countries that perennially outscore the United States, such as Singapore and Japan, are trying to reform their systems to be more like the United States because they recognized the immense damage done by nationalizing their education systems around one set of standards. (See the article by Sophia Tan [2010] for more information on Singapore.)

There are issues that affect test scores at the international level: selective sampling by countries, poverty levels of the students in the samples, opportunity to learn the material on the test, negotiations of actual test questions by the countries involved, culture, and other factors out of the control of schools. For a review of the international tests given since 1964 and the issues associated with student achievement we recommend as a starting point you read Baker (2010) *A Bad Idea: National Standards Based on Test Scores* and Tienken (2008) *Rankings of International Achievement Test Performance and Economic Strength: Correlation or Conjecture?*

Unsubstantiated Rhetoric

Despite 50 years of political noise regarding our imminent demise at the hands of education systems like those of the Soviet Union, Japan, South Korea, and Singapore, our economy has remained the strongest in the world. Although the names have changed recently to China, India, Singapore (again), and sometimes South Korea, the United States still ranks #1 in economic competitiveness.

America has the largest number of students who scored at the top levels in science on the latest PISA for 15-year-olds (OECD, 2009). The United States accounted for 25 percent of the world's top science achievers, almost doubling the next closest competitor, Japan, with only 13 percent, tripling Germany and the United Kingdom, who had only 8 percent of the world's top achievers. Korea had only 5 percent of the world's top achievers, and Hong Kong-China had only 1 percent of the top achievers in science. You'd probably never heard of this achievement, but the information can be found easily online (OECD, 2009).

Keep in mind the U.S. students did not rank in the top spot or even top five on any PISA exam. What is this infatuation on the part of some education leaders and policy makers with nationalizing the curriculum to "do better" on international tests? Is it perhaps PISA envy? We are not sure, but it is not based on empirical evidence (Tienken, 2011).

Protect Local Control and Democracy

Democracy and local control are not standardized, are not efficient, are not easily managed, and their benefits are not easily quantifiable. A democratic education system is not for the faint of heart. It requires constant tending and vigilance. It is not paint-by-numbers.

Education can be a society's greatest democratic gift or a government's greatest undemocratic weapon. Consider the example of China's revolution that began the Mao era in 1949. One of the first things the new communist government did was change the curriculum in all schools. No local control. No provincial input. The centralized government decided for the people what was best based on government's need to control the people.

The Soviets did the same thing when they invaded countries during the 1950s through the 1980s as part of a program known as Russification. History has demonstrated time and time again that a key part of controlling a country's citizenry is through central control of the school curriculum.

National curriculum standards have the power to affect a country's political ideals. Although some supporters of national standards no doubt mean well and care about the country's future, we should all remember the words of Thomas Paine: *The greatest tyrannies are always perpetrated in the name of the noblest causes.* We believe we can do better in the United States than develop and implement policies for our children driven by disinformation, frauds, and anti-intellectualism.

To think that every student in this country should be made to learn the same thing is illogical—it lacks face validity. The United States is just too large and too diverse to engage in such folly. We should have learned from the Soviet Union that central planning does not work in the long run.

The diversity of the United States is one of its greatest strengths. The U.S. economy is able to adapt to change because of the skill diversity of the workforce. The intellectual, creative, and cultural diversity of the U.S. workforce allow it to be nimble and adapt quickly to changes in the marketplace. China, another behemoth of centralization, is trying desperately to crawl out from under the rock of standardization in terms of curriculum and testing (Zhao, 2009) and the effects of those practices on its workforce.

Chinese officials recognize the negative impacts a standardized education system has had on intellectual creativity. Less than 10 percent of Chinese workers are able to function in multinational corporations (Zhao, 2009). I do not know of many Chinese winners of Nobel Prizes in the sciences or in other intellectual fields. China does not hold many scientific patents, and the patents it does hold are of dubious quality (Cyranoski, 2010).

The same holds true for Singapore. Authorities there are have tried several times to move the system away from standardization toward creativity. Standardization and testing are so entrenched in Singapore that every attempt to diversify the system has failed, leaving Singapore a country that has high test scores but no creativity. The problem is so widespread that Singapore must import creative talent from other countries (Tan, 2010).

POINTS TO REMEMBER

The CCCS and the high-stakes testing that will follow represent a formidable tag-team challenge to the unitary system because the dual-system proponents will use the "data" from national tests to show how education is failing. Of course they will not tell the public that many of their standards in math and language arts are developmentally and culturally inappropriate or insensitive. They will simply push numbers to waiting legislators like a drug dealer pushes crack to a junkie. The bifurcation of the system, if allowed to persist, will be complete and irreversible. Just look at China.

REFERENCES

Au, W. (2007). High-Stakes Testing and Curricular Control: A Qualitative Metasynthesis. *Educational Researcher* 36(5): 258–267.

Baker, K. (2010). A Bad Idea: National Standards Based on Test Scores. *AASA Journal of Scholarship and Practice* 7(3): 60–67.

Booher-Jennings, J. (2005). Below the Bubble: "Education Triage" and the Texas Accountability System. *American Education Research Journal* 42(2): 231–268.

Bracey, G. W. (2005). Research: Put Out over PISA. *Phi Delta Kappan* (86)10: 797–798.

Callahan, R. E. (1962). *The Cult of Efficiency.* Chicago: The University of Chicago Press.

Campbell, D. T. (1976, December). *Assessing the Impact of Planned Social Change.* The Public Affairs Center, Dartmouth College, Hanover, NH.

Council of Chief State School Officers. (2009). Standards and accountability. Retrieved from www.ccsso.org/What_We_Do/Standards_Assessment_and_Accountability. html.

Cyranoski, D. (2010, February 15). China's Patent Push. *Nature.* Retrieved from www. nature.com/news/2010/100215/full/news.2010.72.html .

Krueger, A. B. (May, 1999). Experimental estimates of education production functions. *Quarterly Journal of Economics.*

Mathis, W. J. (2010). *The "Common Core" Standards Initiative: An Effective Reform Tool?* Boulder and Tempe: Education and the Public Interest Center & Education Policy Research Unit. Retrieved [July 21, 2010] from epicpolicy.org/publication/common-core-standards.

National Center for Education Statistics. (2008). *The Nation's Report Card: Long Term Trends 2008.* Washington, DC: National Center for Education Statistics, Revised. NCES 2009479.

Organisation for Economic Co-Operation and Development. (2004). *Education at a Glance 2004.* Paris: Author.

Organisation for Economic Co-Operation and Development (OECD). (2009). *Education at a Glance 2009.* Paris: Author.

Ohanian, S. (1999). *One Size Fits Few: The Folly of Educational Standards.* Portsmouth, NH: Heinemann.

Orlich, D. C. (2007). *School Reform: The Great American Brain Robbery.* Frederick, MD: Publish America.

Psacharopoulos, G. & Patrinos, H. A. (2002). " Returns to Investment in Education: A Further Update. " World Bank Working Paper Series, No. 2881. citeseer.ist.psu.edu/psacharopoulos02returns.html.

Piaget, J. (1983). Piaget's Theory. In P. Mussen (ed.). *Handbook of Child Psychology*, 4th ed. Vol. 1. New York: Wiley.

Ramirez, F. O., Luo, X., Schofer, E. & Meyer, J. W. (2006, November). Student Achievement and National Economic Growth. *American Journal of Education*, 113, 1–29.

Sweller, J. (2006). Why Understanding Instructional Design Requires an Understanding of Human Cognitive Evolution. In H. O'Neil & R. Perez (Eds.), Web-Based Learning: Theory, Research, and Practice (pp. 279–295). Hillsdale, NJ: Lawrence Erlbaum Associates, Inc.

Tan, S. (2010). Singapore's educational reforms. The Case for Un-Standardizing Curriculum and Reducing Testing. *AASA Journal of Scholarship and Practice* 6(4): 50–58.

Tanner, D. & L. Tanner. (2007). *Curriculum Development: Theory into Practice*. New York: Allyn & Bacon.

Taylor, F. W. (1947). *Scientific Management*. New York: Harper and Brothers

Tienken, C. H. (2008). Rankings of International Achievement Test Performance and Economic Strength: Correlation or Conjecture. *International Journal of Education Policy and Leadership* 3(4): 1 –15.

Tienken, C. H. (2011, Winter). Common Core State Standards: An example of Data-less Decision-Making. *AASA Journal of Scholarship and Practice* 7(4): 3–18.

Tramaglini, T. (2010). *Student achievement in lower SES high schools*. Unpublished doctoral dissertation, Rutgers University.

Wang, M. C., Haertel, G. D. & Walberg, H. J. (1993). Toward a Knowledge Base for School Learning. *Review of Educational Research*, 63(3): 249–294.

Zagier, A. S. (May 14, 2010). College for All? Experts Say Not Necessarily. AP, Columbia, MO, as reported in the *Spokesman-Review*, p. 2A.

Zhao, Y. (2009). *Catching Up or Leading the Way: American Education in the Age of Globalization*. Alexandria, VA: ASCD.

EIGHT

Charter Schools: Separate but Legal

Up to this point in the book we provided an examination of some threshold events, legislation, and reform-related issues that act as examples of a larger movement and the ways the modern unitary system has come under attack by dual-system proponents, or unwitting accomplices. Beginning with Sputnik and to the Standards Movement 1.0, through NCLB, and now in Standards 2.0 we presented a holistic look at reform.

Although the reform policies and proposals presented thus far attacked either covertly or overtly the unitary system, they only toyed with a concrete dual-system prototype and they did not advocate for the full-scale destruction of the unitary public school system and provide the model; until now.

The charter school movement has grown from a small grassroots effort to improve or provide an option, on a very small scale, to some schools that faced overwhelming odds, to something that is now vended as the panacea to all that supposedly ails public schools. The charter school movement has now been taken over by big business interests and is seen by many as the chance to install the dual system and then move on from there.

IN THE BEGINNING

The Center for Education Reform (2009) reported that there were approximately 5,000 charter schools serving almost 1.5 million students in the United States. The birth of the modern-day charter school "movement," as some supporters like to refer to it, is often credited to University of Massachusetts Amherst professor Ray Budde (Kolderie, 2005). Although Budde was the first to use the term *charter*, Robert Kennedy proposed an

117

idea that we believe to be the modern genesis of the movement in a press release on May 31, 1968 (Guthman & Allen, 1993). Kennedy wrote:

> We must create experimental elementary and secondary schools not run by traditional administrative methods—competitive schools—both as a means for encouraging innovation and as a yardstick for measuring the effectiveness of our schools. (p. 396)

The same basic rhetoric is used today by secretaries of education, legislators, and other charter proponents to forward the charter movement. We are not saying that Robert Kennedy was calling for charter schools specifically, but it does appear at least that the movement co-opted the language he used in this press release to make the case for charters.

The idea picked up steam in 1988 when the president of the American Federation of Teachers, Albert Shanker, supported the idea of establishing schools that were not constrained by the typical state and local bureaucracy and were able to operate semiautonomously both financially and legally. Perhaps Shanker recognized, even 25 years ago, that overregulation and bureaucratization of the public schools by the federal and state governments was constraining innovation and stifling the educational imagination.

However, Shanker (1994) later stepped away from his enthusiastic support of charters when he stated that any common ground that existed between charters and public schools could be wiped out by a large-scale charter movement, along with the unitary system. We wonder what Shanker would think about confluence of pro-charter, anti–public school regulations fostered by NLCB, Race to the Top (RTTT), and the ESEA reauthorization. In some ways Shanker's realization about the dark side of charters was prophetic.

The presidential administrations of Ronald Reagan and George H. W. Bush helped to strengthen the idea of charter schools. Reagan supported vouchers and school choice. Reagan attached the conservative revolution to school choice and provided political strength to supporters of the charter school concept. The Bush I administration, with support from then assistant secretary Diane Ravitch, pushed the choice agenda and rhetoric further. By 1991 the movement was off and running.

Minnesota and California were the first states to adopt charter school legislation in 1991 and 1992 respectively. By the start of school in 2009, 41 states had adopted charter school laws and more were planning to do so in order to be eligible for a portion of the federal 4.3 billion dollar RTTT program. Many states placed caps on the number of charters that could exist, but RTTT guidelines mandated that all caps be lifted.

DEFINED ABOVE THE LAW

Charter schools are legally defined as public schools that are free from some of the financial and regulatory restrictions placed on the unitary public school system. In some respects, they operate outside of the public school system, yet they are marketed as public schools. USCharters-chools.org stated that the three most common reasons to launch a charter school are: (1) Operationalize an educational vision or mission, (2) Increase autonomy from burdensome regulations, and (3) Serve special populations of students. The USDOE explains the purpose of its charter school program on its website, www2.ed.gov/programs/charter/index.html:

> This program provides financial assistance for the planning, program design, and initial implementation of charter schools, and the dissemination of information on charter schools. Grants are available, on a competitive basis, to SEAs in states that have charter school laws; SEAs in turn make subgrants to developers of charter schools who have applied for a charter. If an eligible SEA elects not to participate or if its application for funding is not approved, the Department can make grants directly to charter school developers.
>
> Charter schools provide enhanced parental choice and are exempt from many statutory and regulatory requirements. In exchange for increased flexibility, charter schools are held accountable for improving student academic achievement. The objective is to replace rules-based governance with performance-based accountability, thereby stimulating the creativity and commitment of teachers, parents, and citizens.

So What?

So far things sound pretty innocuous and somewhat helpful on the surface. What a great idea—free schools from overregulation to spur innovation and serve student needs; give parents and students a choice and help those who struggle. But things are not what they seem, once again. What is the connection between charter schools and the marginalization of the unitary system in favor of the expansion of the dual system? What is really going on? Are they really superior, as special interest groups and the USDOE would have you believe?

THE SMOKING GUN

The charter cartel tipped its hand in 2008 when Andy Smarick, formally from the Fordham Foundation and former deputy commissioner at the New Jersey Department of Education, the place we lovingly refer to as the Fairytale Factory, wrote the following tale:

Here, in short, is one roadmap for chartering's way forward: First, commit to drastically increasing the charter market share in a few select communities until it is the dominant system and the district is reduced to a secondary provider. The target should be 75 percent. Second, choose the target communities wisely. Each should begin with a solid charter base (at least 5 percent market share), a policy environment that will enable growth (fair funding, nondistrict authorizers, and no legislated caps), and a favorable political environment (friendly elected officials and editorial boards, a positive experience with charters to date, and unorganized opposition).

Third, secure proven operators to open new schools. To the greatest extent possible, growth should be driven by replicating successful local charters and recruiting high-performing operators from other areas. Fourth, engage key allies like Teach For America, New Leaders for New Schools, and national and local foundations to ensure the effort has the human and financial capital needed. Last, commit to rigorously assessing charter performance in each community and working with authorizers to close the charters that fail to significantly improve student achievement.

As chartering increases its market share in a city, the district will come under growing financial pressure. The district, despite educating fewer and fewer students, will still require a large administrative staff to process payroll and benefits, administer federal programs, and oversee special education. With a lopsided adult-to-student ratio, the district's per-pupil costs will skyrocket.

At some point along the district's path from monopoly provider to financially unsustainable marginal player, the city's investors and stakeholders—taxpayers, foundations, business leaders, elected officials, and editorial boards—are likely to demand fundamental change. That is, eventually the financial crisis will become a political crisis . . . The district could voluntarily begin the shift to an authorizer, developing a new relationship with its schools and reworking its administrative structure to meet the new conditions. Or, believing the organization is unable to make this change, the district could gradually transfer its schools to an established authorizer.

Not so warm and fuzzy, it seems. In fact, if you were to read the full article, and we recommend you do, you will see that Smarick recommends that charters cease cooperation and collaboration with traditional public schools and simply look to replace them. That is exactly what happened in New Jersey. Corporate schooling interests infected the New Jersey Department of Education at the highest levels and began to dismantle the public system, shifting millions in public money to private coffers. Enter the preverbal dual-system dragon.

But what does the research suggest in terms of academic achievement of charter school students? What is that actual effect of choice in terms of the eventual demographic makeup of charter schools and the schools whose students leave to attend charters? What's the underlying philosophy/ies upon which the charter movement and charter school policy is created and implemented? And finally, what really happens when charter schools become a large player in the education sector in terms of the potential for fraud and abuse from the deregulation of a once-stable social institution?

A VISION FOR ACADEMIC EXCELLENCE: WHAT DOES THE RESEARCH SUGGEST?

Supporters of charter schools often cite improved academic performance as a major advantage over traditional public schools. For example, the charter school special interest group Center for Education Reform (2009) published an interesting piece of pseudo research titled *The Accountability Report: Charter Schools*. It's chock-full of methodologically flawed results and conclusions that attempt to make charter schools sound like the magic pill for all that ails student achievement.

Many charter school special interest groups report and publish similar pseudo research. What does the independent research suggest? Reports released since 2005 based on results from national and regional studies show that charter schools offer no significant advantages related to student achievement when controlling for the socioeconomic backgrounds of the students attending the charter schools and their academic achievement prior to entering the charter school.

McEwan (2009) conducted an independent analysis of the report *Everybody Wins: How Charter Schools Benefit All New York City Public School Students* (Winters, 2009) published by the special interest group Center for Civic Innovation at the Manhattan Institute. The analysis revealed no statistically significant gains ($p < .05$) for students as a result of competition from charter schools.

The original report claimed an advantage of 1 percentage point in English language arts test scores for students who left the traditional public school for the charter and an effect size of 0.02 and a statistically insignificant gain of 1 percentage point on the mathematics test scores. To put an effect size of 0.02 in perspective, consider that experimental studies on the effects of class size reduction on student achievement in mathematics and language arts consistently find effects of 0.25 to 0.60 (Egelson & Harman, 2000; Finn & Achilles, 1990).

The independent analysis uncovered issues with the report's claims that the competition posed by charter schools in New York City caused an increase in achievement for low-achieving students who remained in the traditional public schools. The achievement gains were never larger than an effect size of 0.08.

As with other charter-friendly reports, the original report did not acknowledge the confounding variables that could have contributed to the gains, but the independent analysis noted that a short-term decrease in students from the traditional public schools, caused by an exodus to charter schools, can change the peer composition of the public schools.

Achievement could decrease at a school if high achievers leave, and it could increase in the short term if lower-achieving students move to the charter schools. This confounding variable is never discussed in the special interest group report, and the very small, nonsignificant positive results are instead attributed solely to increased competition posed by charter schools. This type of sloppy methodology is characteristic of the many "studies" put out by special interest groups that support charter schools.

Several other methodologically strong studies revealed that the claims made by charter school proponents that charters improve the education for our neediest students are unsubstantiated (Mishel & Roy, 2005; Skinner, 2009; van Lier, 2009). In fact, in most cases, the student populations of many charter schools are not comparable to the schools in the surrounding community (Briggs, 2009). They generally have fewer students eligible for free lunch, and they admit fewer students with special education needs. In a sense, charters are allowed to be semiselective.

Briggs (2009) conducted an independent review of the report published by the RAND Corporation: *Charter Schools in Eight States: Effects on Achievement, Attainment, Integration, and Competition* (Zimmer et al., 2009). The RAND report reviewed student data from jurisdictions in eight states: Texas, Florida, Ohio, Chicago, Denver, Milwaukee, Philadelphia, and San Diego. The report used data from 1994 through the 2007–2008 school years and made the following claims:

- No statistically significant differences in achievement were found in five jurisdictions. Negative achievement differences (charters had lower achievement) were found in Texas and Chicago (data from Florida was excluded from the achievement analysis)
- Charter school performance on statewide tests improves after the first year
- The presence of charters (competition) does not create positive nor negative changes in achievement at the local traditional public schools
- Students who attend charters in Florida and Chicago are significantly more likely to graduate high school and attend two- and four-year colleges
- Charters are not skimming higher-performing students

The independent analysis examined the claims a bit more in-depth and found:

- Findings in the RAND report can only be generalized to students who attend charters in the secondary grades and who transfer to charters from traditional public schools—not the totality of the student population who attend charters.

- The claim that charters create neither positive nor negative changes in the achievement of students in the traditional public schools can only be supported as a short-term claim as RAND did not conduct an analysis that was methodologically strong enough to make long-term claims in this area.

- The claim that charters do not skim students is suggestive and there are not enough data to substantiate the claim further. Curiously, data from other states such as New Jersey and Massachusetts find that charters do skim students.

- There may be a mismatch between the data provided and the statistical methods used to arrive at the finding that students who attend charters in Florida and Chicago are significantly more likely to graduate high school and attend some type of college. Keep in mind that data from most special interest group "research" reports rarely go through an independent peer-review process.

More Shoddy Research from the Charter Crew

Carolyn Hoxby (2004) published two reports on charter achievement that some might consider pseudo research. At the very least, independent analyses have determined those reports to be flawed and overreaching in the conclusions presented. The report that received the most attention, *A Straightforward Comparison of Charter Schools and Public Schools in the United States*, was shown to be anything but straightforward (Mishel & Roy, 2005).

Follow closely and we will take you behind the scenes of the statistical magic that charter school policy charlatans use often to show positive achievement differences favoring charters compared to traditional public schools. Hoxby puts forth the following claims based on her analysis of grade 4 reading and mathematics achievement scores from 99 percent of charter schools:

- Charter school students were 3.8 percent more likely to be proficient in reading
- Achievement is even stronger; 4.9 percent were more likely to be proficient when the racial composition of the charter was similar to that of the local public school
- Charter school students were 1.6 percent more likely to be proficient in math, and that rises to 2.8 percent when "controlling" for student composition in the types of schools
- Claims that "initial indications are that the average student attending a charter school has higher achievement than he or she otherwise would" (p. 3)

Unfortunately, when Mishel and Roy (2005) looked behind the curtain, they found some serious sleight-of hand being conducted in terms of the methods Hoxby used to "compare" the student composition at the charter schools to their local traditional public schools. There were significant demographic differences between the students in the charter schools and those in the "similar" local public schools. This was a classic case of apples versus oranges. As university professors who mentor doctoral students, this issue is something we cover on the first day of the first research methods courses we teach.

Making claims that sound like apples to apples when they are really apples to oranges is a Research 101 No-No. Mishel and Roy (2005) found that the charter school sample used by Hoxby had significantly fewer economically disadvantaged students, 49 percent versus 60 percent for public school. The charter sample had significantly fewer Hispanic students, the lowest-scoring racial group of students on the NAEP assessments, 18 percent versus 30 percent. It had more White students, the second-highest-scoring racial group behind Asians on NAEP assessments, 43 percent versus 36 percent.

Hoxby's sample had a greater percentage of Black students in the sample, and those students historically score higher than Hispanics on NAEP assessments, 34 percent versus 28 percent. The charter schools in Hoxby's study were anything but similar to the traditional public schools she used as the comparison group. Mishel and Roy (2005) went beyond just identifying the errors—they conducted the type of analysis that should have been conducted the first time. Their results are somewhat different than Hoxby's. Below are just a few of the findings from Mishel and Roy's (2005) reanalysis:

- When controlling for the racial composition of the student samples, the math advantage for charters disappears and only charters in California retain a statistically significant advantage in reading, albeit small.
- When controlling for race and economic status, the positive effects for math and reading evaporate.
- In the states where the charter school students were actually similar to those in traditional public schools (Michigan, North Carolina, Ohio, and Texas) the effect of charters on student achievement is negative, but not always statistically significant.
- No attempts to account for selection bias—students who attend charters or their parents CHOOSE to do so. Selection bias is a major threat to the validity of the findings in this case.

Miron, Coryn, and Mackety (2007) conducted an independent analysis of charter school academic performance in the Great Lakes region. The authors used data from Illinois, Indiana, Michigan, Minnesota, Ohio, and Wisconsin. The data suggested that the charters in the region performed at lower levels than demographically similar public schools. Overall, some charters are doing better than predicted, but "nearly two-thirds of the schools have test results lower than predicted" (p. 7).

The authors used the most recent data available that ranged from the 2004–2005 school year to the 2006–2007 school year. Newer charter schools performed worse than established charters. The authors concluded by stating:

> With its longitudinal design, this study has addressed that key area [lack of longitudinal research] and significantly extends the knowledge base available to policymakers. Collectively, the body of evidence presents a mixed picture and provides no clear evidence that charter schools—on the whole—can perform better than traditional public schools. (p. 18)

Hoxby, Murarka, and Kang (2009) produced a report for the New York City Charter Schools Evaluation Project *How New York City's Charter Schools Affect Achievement* that made the following claim, among others: NYC charters schools that students attend for grades kindergarten through 8 closed the rich/poor achievement gap by 66 percent in English language arts (ELA) and 86 percent in math compared to traditional public schools.

That is a potentially stunning claim, given that it seems that charters in New York City were able to almost erase the achievement gap in math and cut it by two-thirds in ELA when most other charters around the country produce achievement gains that are generally identical or lower than those of the traditional public schools. As with the other Hoxby report we presented earlier, this one suffers from some basic methodological flaws along with some more complex issues. Reardon (2009) conducted an independent evaluation of the Hoxby et al. report and found that the above claims, and others made in the report, do not stand up to scrutiny.

Reardon (2009) found in his reanalysis that the students who attend New York City charters are "disproportionately non-Hispanic, black, or poor relative to students in all New York City's schools" (p. 5). Once again, we have apples versus oranges. As for the second claim that the achievement on the Regents exams and the graduate rates are significantly affected, that depends on how one defines statistically significant.

In social science research, it is generally accepted that statistical significance is $p < .05$, or that there is a 95 percent chance that the results obtained did not occur randomly or by chance. Hoxby et al. claim statistical significance at $p < .15$, not even close. Any reputable peer-reviewed research journal would reject such a claim.

A 2009 report for the Center for Research on Education Outcomes (CREDO) reviewed the academic performance of charter school students in 16 states. The report analyzed results from 2,403 charter schools. The main findings related to student achievement were as follows:

- 37 percent of charter schools had achievement that was statistically significantly lower than if their students attended the local traditional public school.
- 17 percent of charter schools had achievement that was statistically significantly higher than if their students attended the local traditional public school.
- 46 percent of charter schools had achievement that was not statistically significantly different from their local traditional public school.
- The learning gains for Blacks and Hispanics are statistically significantly lower than their similar peers in the traditional public schools.

The pooled average achievement for charter schools at the grade 4 level compared to the grade 4 achievement posted on the NAEP in reading and math was -0.01 and -0.03 respectively. The report stated, "Charter school students on average see a decrease in their academic growth in reading of .01 standard deviations compared to their traditional school peers. In math, their learning lags by .03 standard deviations on average. While the magnitude of these effects is small, they are both statistically significant" (p. 12).

The academic results for charter schools in New Jersey are no better than those achieved in other states. Bruce Baker (2009) from Rutgers University conducted an analysis of the 76 charters in operation. The analysis was sponsored by the Education Law Center located in Newark, New Jersey. Baker found, among other things, that:

- The academic performance of New Jersey's charter schools ranks among the lowest in the state.
- As a group, charter schools perform little better than New Jersey's poorest school districts on all statewide tests in grades 3–8 and 11.
- The percentage of students rated as advanced proficient on statewide tests in grades 3–8 and 11 is not much, if any in some cases, better than the percentage of students rated as advanced proficient who attend the poorest schools in the state.
- Students in charter schools are 30 to 35 percent more likely to be in schools where less than 40 percent of the student population is proficient on the statewide tests when compared to students in districts serving lower-middle class students (20 to 30 percent free/reduced lunch population).

Considering that in 2010 New Jersey's governor *at the time* declared open warfare on the state's public schools by cutting funding by over 800 million dollars for the 2010–2011 school year, calling for the lifting of all caps on charter schools, starting an online charter school, and hiring Andy Smarick for a leadership post in the beleaguered New Jersey Department of Education, it seems that Baker's analyses are relevant.

Charters in New Jersey are not performing well, by any stretch, when compared to schools with comparable demographics, yet they are sucking tax money from the traditional public school children: the same public school children that scored at the top reaches of the recent NAEP tests. It is only going to get worse given the proposals to create "Recovery School Districts" in Camden and other struggling cities. We can see the for-profit charter marketeers lining up outside the NJDOE. Well, actually, some of them were employed by the NJDOE as of 2012. So much for conflict of interest rules.

More Evidence?

Bracey (2005) conducted a review of the evidence of charter effectiveness in five states with the largest number of schools: Arizona, California, Illinois, Michigan, North Carolina, and Texas. In all states, as a group, charters did not perform better than the local public schools, and in most cases performed worse.

For example, in North Carolina, students who were in charters had test score gains of 0.10 standard deviations less in reading and 0.16 less in math than when they were in the public schools. If those students remained in charters for five years, the deficit would be at least 0.50 of a standard deviation less gain than if they remained in the public schools.

In Illinois the pass rate of students on the state test for charters hovered around 40 percent for the first three years of the test's administration, whereas it was 60 percent for similar students in the public schools. In Michigan, the results for charters were wildly unstable. For all grades except fourth, the achievement gains for students in charters increased less than the gains for students in the public schools.

Interestingly, the gains for students in charters managed by for-profit education management organizations increased the least. In Texas, the charter school performance was problematic from the beginning. An independent evaluation commissioned by the Texas Education Agency found that only 14 percent of the state's charter schools in 2002 were recognized as high performing, whereas the other 86 percent received low ratings (Texas Center for Educational Research, 2003).

The news was not good for students who attended charter schools for three consecutive years. Students in the public schools outscored their similar peers in the charter schools in math and reading by 16 and 9 scale-score points respectively each year. The achievement picture in California, the state with the country's oldest charter laws dating back to 1992, is just as opaque. Bracey reported that a review in 2003 found that students in charter schools are simply keeping up with their peers, not surpassing, as many advocates of the charter movement promise.

The data from Arizona were even more troubling. Arizona is a "high population" charter environment. An early evaluation of charter school performance conducted in 1999 (Mulholland, 1999) should have rung some alarm bells. The evaluation found that students in charter elementary schools scored similarly to their peers in the public schools, but by middle school gaps began to emerge for students in charters for two or more years.

By high school, those gaps grew to 10 to 15 scale-score points on standardized tests. A study two years later (Solomon, Paark & Garcia, 2001) found that the average effect size of charters on achievement was 0.10, quite small given the effect of other interventions that do not split the unitary system. The independent research we presented relative to charter school academic achievement leaves us wondering, like Bruce Baker at Rutgers, why all the hype?

CHOICE, CHARTER STYLE: SEPARATE, UNEQUAL, AND YET LEGAL

Charter proponents trumpet choice as the hallmark of a democratic public education system. They put a "parent's right to choose" at the forefront of their argument for expanding the charter market and put the parent in the role of consumer. On its face, it sounds very logical. Anything less than free choice would be, of course, un-American. Unless that choice results in an un-American public school stratification.

The argument usually goes something like this: Education is the civil rights issue of our lifetime. Students should not be made to attend schools that are persistently unsafe and that do not deliver a quality education. Parents should have the right to choose a school that is right for their child. Sounds very democratic and consumer-chic, yes?

Now consider this: By allowing people to choose (and not everyone chooses to leave or has access to the information needed to make a good choice), there is potential, in a weakly regulated system, for certain parents to choose certain schools based on factors that create greater segregation along academic, racial, ethnic, special education, or socioeconomic lines, or combinations of factors, than existed in the traditional public school.

There is also the certainty that the public school will lose much-needed funding because every child that goes to the charter school takes a majority of his or her per-pupil funding with him/her—thus effectively creating a public dual system based on the all-American right of free choice. But what does the research suggest?

We are not far off with our modest example. Results from several large studies demonstrate that in many cases the students in charter schools either come from homes that are more economically stable, have higher prior achievement levels, do not require special education, ELL, or intense medical services, and exhibit patterns of white-flight or minority flight from the public school to the charter.

The charter sector itself is segregated. For example, Fuller et al. (2003) reported that charter schools with higher proportions of minority students, on average, have fewer overall resources and weaker academic programs than do charters that serve a majority White student population. Moreover, charter schools have less diverse student populations in terms of socioeconomics than their peer public schools. Ascher et al., (1999) reported at the time that only 35 percent of charters, compared to over 70 percent of public schools, had economically diverse populations.

This means that charters serve primarily poor or nonpoor students, or primarily non-White students, in more cases than public schools that serve very economically and demographically mixed populations in a majority of the schools. Some of you might be saying, "Well that was in 1999, things have matured since then." Consider that Miron et al. (2010) found the same level of economic concentration and segregation in 2010. So much for growing older and wiser.

The Miron et al. study found several interesting aspects of charters and segregation: (a) only about 25 percent of charter schools operated by education management organizations (EMOs) had a student population demographically similar to that of the surrounding public schools; (b) charters administered by EMOs had extreme levels of economic segregation: either very wealthy or very poor; (c) charter schools, as a whole, enroll fewer students with special needs than the surrounding public schools; (d) charter schools provide fewer special education services, and in some cases do not have to provide services if special education is not part of their mission (Howe & Welner, 2002); (e) virtual charter school students are likely to be White and not economically disadvantaged.

Of course, not all charters segregate in every situation, but as a group, their student populations are more segregated than the surrounding public schools. There are charters that are more inclusive, less segregated, and offer better programs than their surrounding schools, but that is not the overall characteristic of the population of charter schools.

But don't be fooled by misleading or incomplete statistics. For example, in 2001, 33 percent of all students in charter schools were Black, whereas only 17 percent of students in public schools were Black. Seems like charters are more inclusive and do serve a larger minority population. That is good, right? Maybe, as it depends on your goal. But consider this: Over 70 percent of Black students in charter schools were in schools that were 90 to 100 percent Black, lacking almost any racial diversity, whereas only 34 percent of Black students in the public schools were in

schools that were 90 to 100 percent all Black (Frankenberg, 2011; Frankenberg & Lee, 2003).

We think it is important to remember that at various times in our
country's history people have "chosen" to keep slaves, not allow women
to vote, create separate and unequal facilities for non-White citizens, institute voting laws to make it difficult for certain citizens to vote, restrict
who can get married, and to ban bilingual education, to name a few
things. All in the name of liberty and a person's right to choose.

Choice for choice's sake is irresponsible, reckless, and in some cases,
undemocratic. Passing laws and policies that have now been shown to
weaken the democratic fabric of the country by facilitating people's
choice to segregate is immoral, and those who knowingly create and
support such laws and policies are engaging in social and moral malpractice.

Students in public schools attend more racially diverse schools, on
average, than their peers in charter schools. If your goal is to facilitate the
siloing of students, and thus eventually society, by race, ethnicity,
achievement, special needs and ELL status, and economics, all based on
the "free choice" of parents supported by law, then charters are good.

If your goal is a unitary system in which people of all races, ethnic-
ities, economic levels, languages, special needs, and cognitive backgrounds learn, collaborate, and deliberate together side-by-side in the
rich pool of diversity, then charters are not so good. What's healthier in
the long run for a democracy? We argue for the second, the more diverse
(in every sense of the word) option.

Selection Bias

It is important to enter into the record the fact that some charter
schools practice selective admissions. Yes, we know that is illegal and
that in most states charter schools must hold lotteries to admit students—
and they do. The issue is what happens after lottery. The first author has
had private discussions with the heads of multiple charter schools about
their admissions practices in an attempt to determine why charter school
populations differ so much from their local public schools in terms of the
percentage of students with special needs and ELLs. The charter heads
represented schools that spanned the K-12 spectrum.

The scenario generally goes something like this: (1) All students who
win the lottery must fill out a detailed student intake form. The form
requires parents to disclose any special needs the child might have and in
some cases free/reduced lunch status; (2) Parents and students must sub-
mit to an "intake interview" with the leadership of the charter school to
be oriented to the "expectations" of the school; (3) In some schools, students must produce a writing sample; (4) Students who have special
needs, behavior issues, are ELLs, or possess other factors that might in-

fluence achievement negatively, are gently counseled about the possible mismatch between their needs and the school's mission.

In some cases parents are told that their student might not fit the school or that the school does not offer the level of service needed. They might also be made to feel uncomfortable or not quite the type of clientele served by the school. It is similar to the situation in some communities of the country when an African American couple go house shopping and they are shown homes in one section of town and not another, or dissuaded from purchasing a home in a traditional White middle-class neighborhood. Yes, that still happens.

Of course not all charter schools participate in selective admissions counseling. Some other reasons why charter schools generally have more favorable student demographics are that the poorest of the poor parents have less means (time, money, information, support) to make informed choices or to get their students to the new school. New schools sometimes mean new schedules, which in turn means new child care, a scarce commodity for the poor. Selective admission policies only exacerbate an already troubling situation.

Data

By law the school has to fit the child, not the other way around. If the charter school does not offer the special education service currently, it must to meet the needs of the child. The fact that the school might not want to offer the service or does not currently is immaterial. Subtly counseling parents to rethink their choice is illegal and immoral, but difficult to prove. Creating an uninviting environment during an intake interview in hopes that a parent will not choose to send her child with special needs to the charter is immoral, unethical, and undemocratic. But it happens.

Do you think that everyone has the same access to the information and resources necessary to make an appropriate choice about schooling? Does everyone have the resources necessary to get their children to another school? How do people without cars and daily access to the Internet get their information and their children to schools?

Think we are overhyping this? Take New Jersey for example, a charter school hotbed. The data there, compiled by Bruce Baker (2009; 2010) from Rutgers University in New Jersey, demonstrated our point. Baker showed by using GIS mapping software and free lunch data from the National Center of Education Statistics Common Core of Data that as a group, the charter schools in Newark and Jersey City enroll almost half as many students eligible for free lunch.

The distinction between being eligible for free lunch as opposed to reduced lunch is important here. Free lunch is a statistically significant reducer of achievement on standardized tests. Children eligible for free lunch represent the poorest of the poor, the most economically fragile of children.

Baker (2009; 2010) also demonstrated that charter schools in Newark and Jersey City enroll 40 percent to 90 percent fewer students with special needs other than speech (a lower-level need). For example, in 2007, two of the "nationally recognized" charter schools in Newark, Robert Treat Academy and North Star Academy, enrolled 3.8 percent and 7.8 percent of students with disabilities (excluding speech), compared to 18.1 percent for the Newark Public Schools.

Thus, we have a situation in the state's two largest cities where a dual system exists. The first system is for less-poor and non/less-disabled students, whereas the public school system is being turned into a catch basin for our neediest and most fragile children. That's an interesting way to build a national reform model, unless you are building the education version of Halliburton, Enron, TYCO, Global Crossing, Arthur Andersen, or any of the multitude of big businesses that have defrauded the public in the last 15 years. Yes, education Enron—that fits.

Separation of Church and State? Not Quite

A quiet trend is taking place within the charter movement: blurring the lines between church and state. There are currently charter schools that focus on Turkish language and culture, Hebrew language and culture, and some charters are housed in Christian church buildings. Charter schools devoted to other languages and cultures also exist, all publicly funded. This creates the context in which covert or subtle religious instruction or indoctrination can take place.

Now we have a potential situation in which religion can be brought covertly into the public school classroom through the study of culture and language. It is very hard to separate Hebrew language and culture from Judaism or Turkish language and culture from aspects of Islam. In terms of housing charter schools founded by Christian church pastors in church-owned buildings . . . well, we will let you reflect on that one a bit (Tienken, 2011).

The Turkish language and cultural schools in particular have raised some concerns in the past five years. Many of the over 100 Turkish language and culture schools that service over 35,000 students have financial and philosophical connections to Fethullah Gulen. Gulen, a Turkish nationalist now living in exile in Pennsylvania, is well known for proposing that Islam should take greater precedence in Turkish society.

Gulen-affiliated or -inspired groups operate schools in 25 states. Although most Gulen-inspired schools distance themselves from the exiled nationalist, the money flows from those committed to his teachings into organizations that support the charter schools. This creates the ability to purchase influence. Some of these Turkish language and culture schools have been cited for crossing the line between church and state.

In Minnesota the Tarek ibn Ziyad Academy authorized by the Islamic Relief USA organization was cited by state education officials for having teachers take part in Friday prayers voluntarily. Regardless of the ties to the money, the association with the philosophical teachings of Gulen is troubling given that participative democracy is not the hallmark of the philosophy (Tienken, 2011).

Questions also surround the Hebrew language and culture charter schools that have opened in New York City and Florida. In the case of New York, Diane Ravitch (January 18, 2009) described a situation surrounding the opening of the Hebrew Language Academy Charter School in Brooklyn, New York, funded in part by Michael Steinhardt. Steinhardt is known as a philanthropist who has donated millions of dollars to promote Jewish culture and identity. Ravitch wrote:

> His generosity is unquestionable. In this case, however, he is asking taxpayers to support an institution that has obvious religious overtones. In a city with a great variety of Jewish schools and other agencies that encourage Jewish identity, it makes no sense to create a public school with the same purpose . . . The proposal to the Regents asserts that the school will not engage in any devotional activities. Even so, the Hebrew language is so closely aligned with the Jewish religion that it is baffling that the Regents are willing to treat the proposed charter school as a nonsectarian institution.

The Hebrew Language Academy charter school is another example of a school that raises some questions in terms of blurring the lines between church and state. On its website one can find students waving Israeli flags, Israeli flags hanging throughout classrooms, and teachers' classrooms are given Hebrew names such as Hertzeliya, an Isreali city named after Theodor Herzl, the founder of modern Zionism. Another classroom with the name Eilat is another city and is also known for being part of the Book of Exodus.

Yet another classroom name, Netanya, means, among other things, "God has given." As Ravitch stated, it is very difficult to separate Hebrew language and culture from religion. The Hebrew culture is rich with history, and much of that history revolves around religion. Consider a charter school with classrooms named Peter the Fisherman, or Martin Luther, or the Garden of Eden. See the potential problem here?

Our purpose is not to single out three specific religions or cultures. There exist Chinese, Haitian, Austrian, Korean, and other such language and culture charters in the United States. Our purpose is to provide examples of how allowing specific cultural charters can facilitate the blurring of the lines between church and state. As Ravitch noted, it is difficult to separate the Hebrew language and culture from the Jewish religion.

More important, publicly funding, encouraging, and supporting through policy schools with such a narrow focus brings us further and further away from the original unifying vision of Jefferson, Mann, Parker, Dewey, and the other giants who supported and built the democratic, unified, public school system.

The Final Word on Separate, Unequal, and Legal

Frankenberg and Lee (2003) stated it clearly and in language we believe is easy to understand. There is something undemocratic and fundamentally unethical going on here. Public tax dollars are once again being used to tier the social system, through the legal and education systems:

> The justification for segregated schools as places of opportunity is basically a "separate but equal" justification, an argument that there is something about the schools that can and does overcome the normal pattern of educational inequality that afflicts many of these schools. Charter school advocates continually assert such advantages and often point to the strong demand for the schools by minority parents in minority communities, including schools that are designed specifically to serve a minority population. . . . Unfortunately, despite claims by charter advocates, there is no systematic research or data that show that charter schools perform better than public schools. (p. 3)

So now we are left in a situation in which the struggling school loses funding; is more racially, academically, or ethnically segregated; and based on the evidence, loses some of its more involved, economically more stable parents. In essence, the charter school then facilitates greater segregation across a variety of lines and takes money away from a school that probably needs it, leaving the kids who are left in the public school in a more segregated situation without the funding they need to do better or receive better programs or upgrade security. Now, that sounds somewhat un-American.

UNDERLYING PHILOSOPHY OF CHARTER SCHOOLS

The original charter school movement, the one driven by local needs, has since been replaced by a new movement, Charter 2.0 if you will. This new charter movement is personified by the ideas of those like Andy Smarick: marketize the system, marginalize local public schools and local control of local tax dollars, and install a tiered system of for-profit and publicly funded schools. But where do these types of ideas emanate from? What is the philosophical underpinning for such a system, and is that congruent with the Jeffersonian view of education, or an equitable view of public schools as a vehicle to realizing liberty and justice for all?

One must be able to identify and understand the underlying philosophy/ies upon which reform proposals stand, to be able to truly understand the reform. If one does not understand from where the ideas come, one cannot understand truly the ideas, and thus, will not understand the intended and unintended consequences of the policies built upon the ideas. The current charter school movement is built upon a mix of postmodern consumerism and neoliberalism. Knowing that allows us to examine the philosophies to find the weaknesses and concerns.

Neoliberalism

Neoliberalism is a philosophy born out of an economic ideology that free market competition and privatization of state social services is a more efficient and effective way to run a society (Steger & Roy, 2010). Neoliberal policy makers believe that the state should not be involved in providing social services. Proponents believe that the state's role should be limited to the organization of outsourcing those services to private companies. Deregulation, tax decreases for the wealthiest citizens, opposition to unions, unrestrained capitalism, and fostering work insecurity to lower labor costs are some hallmarks of the philosophy (Bourdieu, 1999).

In education, neoliberal policies include (a) allowing public tax dollars to be used to fund private school tuition through vouchers or tax credits to families who send their students to school outside of the public system, (b) the creation of semiprivate schools, known as charter schools, run by private companies, private boards of interested parties, or education management organizations funded by public tax dollars, (c) cutting state funding to public schools in order to foster privatization, (d) encouraging the elimination of teachers' unions in order to subvert the collective bargaining process, and (e) encouraging merit pay based on the results from one statewide standardized test.

One result of neoliberal education policy is the creation of a two-tiered system, ripe for privatization and thus a potential cash cow for the private sector, but a loss for the common citizen and child. It is social Darwinism played out in schools: Those who already come with the most wealth, get the most quality.

Postmodern Consumerism

Aggressive marketing and a zealous attempt to manufacture new capitalist markets are two hallmarks of postmodern consumerism. The felt needs and desires of the individual trump the social needs of the greater population. Personal choice rules, and there is not a shortage of must-have products marketed to create those felt needs (Corrigan, 1998). Success is measured by consumption and the accumulation of material goods, at any cost. Consuming becomes the way people self-identify in postmodern consumerism (Jessup, 2001).

Truth becomes marginalized within the growing space of the market. Product marketing replaces empirical fact in an effort to drive consumption and increase it. Think of new car marketing or cell phone marketing campaigns. Now transfer that type of marketing to schooling—it's coming. It's already here in some markets. Some of you might still be saying—yes, that is good because it offers choice.

Now consider this: Does everyone who is marketed new cars or cell phones have equal access to every car or cell phone for which they are marketed? No. It is one thing to be marketed a high-end luxury car and a whole other to actually be able to afford to CHOOSE that car, or in the case of some charter schools, for you to be chosen for that car.

The convergence of neoliberalism and postmodern consumerism creates a fertile field for big business to become more financially involved in the movement. It's a perfect fit for speculation, market manipulation, and new market creation. Therefore it is no wonder there has been a surge in the amount of money invested by big business in the movement.

BIG BUSINESS ENTERS THE BUILDING

It only makes sense that a movement with roots in neoliberal postmodern consumerism would sooner or later be influenced, if not in some ways hijacked, by big business. For-profit EMOs like Connection Academy, K-12 Inc., Edison Schools, National Heritage Academies, Imagine Schools, Inc., Charter Schools USA, and White Hat Management are some of the largest for-profit corporations managing charter schools. As of 2008 there were 50 EMOs operating in 28 states with over 250,000 students enrolled. (Molnar, Miron & Urschel, 2008).

Remember, those are for-profit operations. Their objective is to make money. That raises the possibility that decisions will be made based first on the effect on profits, not children. The information to support our claim is not hard to locate. Finding the scandals is easy enough. Simply search on the Internet for things like "White Hat Management and Scandal" (e.g., charterschoolscandals.blogspot.com/2010/05/white-hat-management.html), or "Edison Learning School Management and Scandal" (e.g., www.pasasf.org/edison/pdfs/042105.pdf), or any of the large for-profit EMOs and the term *scandal*. We find White Hat a model scandal in terms of what will happen across the country as charter schools proliferate in the landscape—well worth the reading.

But there is another major player besides EMOs: big banks. Yes, they are back fresh off their victory from the 2008 worldwide economic catastrophe that the taxpayers will own for many years to come. Big banks are now in the charter school start-up business, and business is booming. It seems as if there is money to be made in financing charter schools. Big banks are hurtling themselves into the market with tens and hundreds of millions of dollars at a time.

Big banks are actively campaigning and buying off legislators to help feed the charter frenzy. Trip Gabriel and Jennifer Medina (May 9, 2010) wrote an exposé in the *New York Times* explaining what is going on.

> Wall Street has always put its money where its interests and beliefs lie. But it is far less common that so many financial heavyweights would adopt a social cause like charter schools and advance it with a laserlike focus in the political realm. Hedge fund executives are thus emerging as perhaps the first significant political counterweight to the powerful teachers unions, which strongly oppose expanding charter schools in their current form. They have been contributing generously to lawmakers in hopes of creating a friendlier climate for charter schools. More immediately, they have raised a multimillion-dollar war chest to lobby this month for a bill to raise the maximum number of charter schools statewide to 460 from 200. The money has paid for television and radio advertisements, phone banks and some 40 neighborhood canvassers in New York City and Buffalo—all urging voters to put pressure on their lawmakers.

Gabriel and Medina describe in their article the current environment, fed by a little-known law signed in 1999 by then President Clinton and passed by the Republican Congress, that allows banks to cash in on up to 39 percent tax credits for financing the creation of "new markets." Charter schools qualify as a new market. Juan Gonzalez (May 7, 2010) reported on this phenomena through the microcosm of Albany, New York.

> Wealthy investors and major banks have been making windfall profits by using a little-known federal tax break to finance new charter-school construction. The program, the New Markets Tax Credit, is so lucrative that a lender who uses it can almost double his money in seven years.
>
> Under the New Markets program, a bank or private equity firm that lends money to a nonprofit to build a charter school can receive a 39 percent federal tax credit over seven years. The credit can even be piggybacked on other tax breaks for historic preservation or job creation. By combining the various credits with the interest from the loan itself, a lender can almost double his investment over the seven-year period. No wonder JPMorgan Chase announced this week it was creating a new $325 million pool to invest in charter schools and take advantage of the New Markets Tax Credit. Albany is exhibit A in the web of potential conflicts that keep popping up in the charter school movement. . . . If wealthy investors and banks can double their money simply by building charter schools, taxpayers deserve to know exactly who arranged those deals, who will benefit and what they will ultimately cost each school.

In an economic environment where most of those big banks are paying as little as 1.25 percent for a rate of return on a one-year certificate of deposit, doubling my money in just seven years sounds like a good deal to me. Unfortunately, you and I are not eligible for that deal. We're stuck with the 1.25 percent, and we get to fund the interest and principal payments those charter schools must make to the big banks. So that's how the new dual system works: interesting.

POINTS TO REMEMBER

Perhaps charter schools are not the answer to improving public education. Creating a multitiered, balkanized education system will not solve the problems we face as a society. It seems that charter schools fall flat in terms of achieving their stated goals of superior achievement. They can't overcome the drag on learning caused by having children born into and grow up in conditions similar to those found in developing countries.

Charter schools can't overcome broken housing policy that favors the nonpoor (Schwartz, 2010), broken health policy that allows indigent pregnant women to be denied consistent health care, and fiscal policies that keep low wage earners in low-wage jobs with no way to pay their children's way out of poverty. It seems to us that a unitary system, supported by a unitary social system, is the best way to raise student achievement and more important, a way to build a compassionate, participative democracy. But as we stated in the first chapter, we are biased in favor of such a democracy.

A LOOK AHEAD

In the final chapter we provide our ideas for reform. As can be expected, we do not provide a recipe. Instead, we provide some guiding ideas that others can use to create customized reform proposals. One will notice that the higher up the bureaucratic food chain we go, the more general the ideas. That is because we do not believe that distal bureaucrats should be creating specific regulations and mandating specific practices at the local level. Local control of curriculum and instruction is just that: local control.

REFERENCES

Ascher, C., Jacobowitz, R. & McBride, Y. (1999). *Standards-based reform and the charter school movement in 1998–99: An analysis of four states.* New York University, Institute for Education and Social Policy.

Baker, B. (2009). NJ Charters: Worthy of the Hype? Education Law Center: Newark, NJ.

Baker, B. (2010). More fun with New Jersey charter schools. Schoolfinance101. Retrieved from: schoolfinance101.wordpress.com/2010/01/26/more-fun-with-new-jersey-charter-schools/.

Bracey, G. (2005). Charter Schools Performance and Accountability: A Disconnect. Boulder and Tempe: Education and the Public Interest Center & Education Policy Research Unit. Retrieved from www.epicpolicy.org/files/EPSL-0505-113-EPRU.pdf.

Briggs, D. C. (2009). Review of Charter Schools in Eight States: Effects on Achievement, Attainment, Integration and Competition. Boulder and Tempe: Education and the Public Interest Center & Education Policy Research Unit. Retrieved from epicpolicy.org/thinktank/review-Charter-Schools-Eight-State.

Bourdieu, P. (1999). *The Weight of the World: Social Suffering in Contemporary Society.* Oxford, UK: Polity.

Center for Education Reform. (2009). Retrieved from www.edreform.com/Fast_Facts/Ed_Reform_FAQs/?Just_the_FAQs_Charter_Schools.

Corrigan, P. (1998). *The Sociology of Consumption.* London: Sage Publications.

Center for Research on Education Outcomes (CREDO). (2009). Multiple choice: Charter school performance in 16 states. Author. Retrieved from credo.stanford.edu/reports/MULTIPLE_CHOICE_CREDO.pdf.

Egelson, P. & Harman, P. (2000). Ten Years of Small Class Sizes in Burke County, North Carolina. In Margaret C. Wang and Jeremy D. Finn (Eds.), *How Small Classes Help Teachers Do Their Best* (pp. 279–297), Philadelphia: Temple University Center for Research in Human Development and Education.

Finn, J. D. & Achilles, C. M. (1990). Answers and Questions about Class Size: A Statewide Experiment. *American Educational Research Journal* 27: 557–577.

Frankenberg, E. (2011). Educational Charter Schools: A Civil Rights Mirage? *Kappa Delta Pi Record* 47(3): 100–105.

Frankenberg, E. & Lee, C. (2003, September 5). Charter Schools and Race: A Lost Opportunity for Integrated Education. *Education Policy Analysis Archives,* 11(32). Retrieved from epaa.asu.edu/epaa/v11n32/.

Fuller, B., Gawlik, M., Gonzales, E. K. & Park, S. (2003, April). Charter schools and inequality: Policy analysis for California education. Retrieved from pace.berkeley.edu/Chartersummary.pdf.

Gabriel, T. & Medina, J. (2010, May 9). Charter Schools' New Cheerleaders: Financiers. *New York Times.* Retrieved from: www.nytimes.com/2010/05/10/nyregion/10charter.html?hp.

Gonzalez, J. (2010, May 7). Albany Charter Cash Cow: Big Banks Making a Bundle on New Construction as Schools Bear the Cost. *NY Daily News.* www.nydailynews.com/ny_local/education/2010/05/07/2010-05-07_albany_charter_cash_cow_big_banks_making_a_bundle_on_new_construction_as_schools.html .

Guthman, E. O. & Allen, R. C. (1993). *RFK: Collected Speeches.* New York, NY: Penguin Books.

Howe, K. R. & Welner, K. G. (2002). School Choice and the Pressure to Perform: Deja Vu for Children with Disabilities? *Remedial and Special Education* 23(4): 212–21.

Hoxby, C. M. (2004, September). *A Straightforward Comparison of Charter Schools and Regular Public Schools in the United States.* The National Bureau of Economic Research, 1–23.

Hoxby, C. M., Murarka, S. & Kang, J. (2009, September). "How New York City's Charter Schools Affect Achievement." Second report in series. Cambridge, MA: New York City Charter Schools Evaluation Project, September 2009. Retrieved October 1, 2009, from www.nber.org/~schools/charterschoolseval/.

Jessup, M. (2001). Truth: The First Casualty of Postmodern Consumerism. *Christian Scholar's Review* 30(3): 289–304.

Kolderie, T. (2005, June). Ray Budde and the Origins of the Charter Concept. *Education Evolving.* Retrieved from www.educationevolving.org/pdf/Ray_Budde.pdf.

McEwan, P. J. (2009). Review of *Everyone Wins: How Charter Schools Benefit All New York City Public School Students*. Boulder and Tempe: Education and the Public Interest Center & Education Policy Research Unit.

Miron, G., Coryn, C. & Mackety, D. M. (2007). *Evaluating the impact of charter schools on student achievement: A longitudinal look at the Great Lakes States*. The Evaluation Center, Western Michigan University, Kalamazoo, MI.

Miron, G., Urschel, J. L., Mathis, W. J. & Tornquist, E. (2010). *Schools without Diversity: Education Management Organizations, Charter Schools and the Demographic Stratification of the American School System*. Boulder and Tempe: Education and the Public Interest Center & Education Policy Research Unit. Retrieved from nepc.colorado. edu/publication/schools-without-diversity.

Mishel, L. & Roy, J. (2005). *Re-examining Hoxby's Findings of Charter School Benefits*. Washington, DC: Economic Policy Institute.

Molnar, A., Miron, G. & Urschel, J. (2008). Profiles of for-profit educational management organizations: Tenth annual report. Education in the Public Interest Center. Boulder, CO. nepc.colorado.edu/publication/profiles-profit-education-management-organizations-2007-2008.

Mulholland, L. A. (1999). Arizona charter school progress evaluation. Tempe, AZ: Morrison Institute, Arizona State University, p. 26.

Ravitch, D. (2009, January 18). New Schools Flunk the Unity Test. *New York Daily News*. Retrieved from: www.nydailynews.com/opinions/2009/01/18/2009-01-18_new_school_flunks_unity_test_hebrewlangu.html.

Reardon, S. F. (2009). *Review of "How New York City's Charter Schools Affect Achievement."* Boulder and Tempe: Education and the Public Interest Center & Education Policy Research Unit. Retrieved from epicpolicy.org/thinktank/review-How-New-York-City-Charter.

Schwartz, H. (2010). *Housing Policy is School Policy: Economic Integrative Housing Promotes Academic Success in Montgomery County, Maryland*. New York: The Century Foundation.

Shanker, A. (1994). *Where We Stand: The Chicago Reform*. Washington D.C.: American Federation of Teachers.

Skinner, K. J. (2009). *Charter School Success or Selective Out-Migration of Low Achievers*. Boston: Massachusetts Teachers Association.

Smarick, A. (2008, Winter). Wave of the Future: Why Charters Should Replace Failing Urban Schools. *Education Next* 8(1). educationnext.org/wave-of-the-future/.

Solomon, L., Paark, K. & Garcia, D. (2001). *Does Charter School Attendance Improve Test Scores? The Arizona Results*. Phoenix, AZ: The Center for Market-Based Education, the Goldwater Institute, p. 4.

Steger, M. B. & Roy, R. V. (2010). *Neoliberalism: A Very Short Introduction*. Oxford, UK: Oxford University Press.

Texas Center for Educational Research. (2003, July). Texas Open-Enrollment Charter Schools: Sixth Year Evaluation. Austin, TX: Author.

Tienken, C. H. (2011, Fall). The Expanding Charter Movement: Separate, Unequal, and Legal? *AASA Journal of Scholarship and Practice* 8(3): 3–11.

Uscharterschools.org. Retrieved from www.uscharterschools.org/pub/uscs_docs/o/index.htm.

U.S. Department of Education. *Charter school program state education agencies (SEA) grant*. Retrieved from www2.ed.gov/programs/charter/index.html.

U.S. Department of Education. A Commitment to Quality: National Charter School Policy Forum Report, Washington, D.C., 2008. Retrieved from www2.ed.gov/admins/comm/choice/csforum/report.pdf.

van Lier, P. (2011, May 17). Testimony of Piet van Lier, Senior Researcher, before the Senate Finance Committee. Policy Matters Ohio. Retrieved from www.policymattersohio.org/wp-content/uploads/2011/10/PvanLierHB153Testimony2011_0517.pdf.

Zimmer, R., Gill, B., Booker, K., Lavertu, S., Sass, T. R., & White, J. (2009). Charter schools in eight states. Effects on achievement, attainment, integration, and competition. Rand Corporation.

NINE

What Now? A Way Forward

Policy makers and education critics in the United States have a history of using myth, fear, and falsehoods to attack the unitary system. In this book we presented some examples that highlight those practices. However, this period in time appears to be different from the reform initiatives of decades past.

Until now, the system would bend, but not break. But the introduction of NCLB, Common Core State Standards, national testing, Race to the Top, the ESEA reauthorization, and the convergence of neoliberal market policies that now flow out of Democratic and Republican think tanks and policy conventions have inflicted deep wounds on what is considered by most free countries as the greatest education system on the planet.

Vouchers, charter schools, big business privatization, and lies are all being used to separate the people from their system, and in the process, replace the Jeffersonian vision of a unitary public school with a two-tiered, separate, but legally unequal brand of edu-corporation education. The system is in danger of collapsing, and with it will collapse one of the citizenry's pieces of democracy that they still control locally.

How has this been allowed to happen? In our opinion two groups have been complicit in the bludgeoning of America's free and democratic unitary system.

1. SOME RANK AND FILE EDUCATORS

As a group, educators have played a role in this, the real crisis in education; the destruction of the unitary system. Although there have been strong voices against destruction, the rank and file of the occupation have not used their collective influence to develop a clear message and targeted strategy to save and improve the system. Some have not informed

143

themselves beyond the surface noise that consumes education policy debates. Some of our colleagues do not seem to be overly supportive or vocal in favor of a strong unitary system.

They seem not to understand the ongoing fight for the unitary system, why it is important in the preservation of local control, liberty and justice for all students, and democracy. Too often educators repeat the myths of Sputnik, "lagging behind other countries," and the need for national standards and testing. Some have not read the seminal works of their occupation and some too easily follow their national associations into the world of data-less decision making.

As Callahan (1962) described so eloquently and completely, the administrative core of education association leaders consists of a group of business wannabes who lead their people over the cliff so as to receive affirmation from their corporate idols. Take for example the number of national and state education associations selling products and services related to the unquestioning implementation of the Common Core State Standards. Some association leaders never stopped to ask why. They simply jumped to product development and sales marketing to those in their associations whom they were to serve and support. Education professionals have a history of not asking why.

As a group, the professional education associations and some educators embraced Frederick Taylor's scientific management principles and the efficiency movement over 100 years ago. This movement was born out of shoveling coal and the metallurgy process, and some education leaders wholeheartedly brought that concept into the classrooms and mechanized school and childhood. We have been trying to jettison these practices ever since. Are the CCSS and national testing just scientific management 2.0?

This is not to say that ALL educators and ALL association leaders are complicit. They are certainly not. There are many who understand the issues, fight for children and a free and democratic unitary system, and put their professional reputations on the line resisting and defying the myths, fear, and lies. You know the people of whom we speak. They are the lone voices at the meetings who ask questions about the efficacy of policies. They ask why. They request evidence, and they wonder aloud how certain policies are going to affect children. They question the policy makers and those misguided educrats who attempt to force them to implement the bankrupt policies.

These are the people who stand up to the system while 20 other people sit around the conference table and say nothing or don't question the policies, and never ask why. It is very difficult for these defenders of the unitary system to gain traction when their peers follow the other lemmings into certain demise. But yet they persist to resist. For that we are grateful and we stand with you.

2. POLICY MAKERS

Some policy makers have been disappointing in their ability to make decisions in the best interest of children. Although many have made their voice heard, they are overpowered by the sound of cash registers. We believe that it is money that makes decisions in this reform environment, but it seems more obscene now. One needs to look only at the growth of charter schools and the for-profit education sector since 2008 to see how money has been able to buy votes for charters and corporate education management companies.

In our opinion the best examples of this are in Ohio and New Jersey, although it is now happening across the country. The primary charter school law that got the ball rolling in Ohio came about because one of the major for-profit providers of online charter schools was a heavy political donor to the key players in the Ohio assembly. That donor runs an empire of online charter schools that takes millions of dollars in taxpayer money but is not accountable for results. Ohio is flooded with low-quality charter schools thanks to campaign contributions. By the time the citizens of Ohio woke up, their public schools were fleeced, and the local decision-making power was whisked away to the private sector.

In true New Jersey style, politics and personal connections grease the skids. New Jersey is now in a unique position. Its top education leadership are former corporate members of for-profit education management organizations and charter school associations. They pursue money from hedge-fund managers and social networking website owners to support the privatization of New Jersey's schools.

Of course we are not saying that the top leaders of New Jersey's education apparatus have conflicts or financial interests in any way that influence their decision making. We are saying that the charter movement and education management movement in New Jersey has deep pockets, and when the smoke clears, we believe that some policy makers will have had their hands down low in those pockets. Readers are encouraged to find the investigative stories published by Bob Braun since 2011 that detail the New Jersey edu-politics playing out and judge for themselves.

WHAT WE KNOW

The Economics of It All

By now it should be well known that the NCLB reforms actually slowed the academic progress being made by the major subgroups of students when compared to a similar time span prior to the law being implemented (Fuller et al., 2007). Yet reforms being vended by opinion makers call for an extension of the same type of policies through national standards, national testing, merit pay, vouchers, charter schools, and other distractions. In this section we present some ideas for policy makers and educators to consider and attempt to support.

Educators and policy makers have to stop spreading the myths, fear, and lies about American education "lagging" behind other countries. We demonstrated repeatedly in this book that those myths don't stand up to empirical scrutiny. The problem is that some educators and policy makers do not scrutinize the headlines, and instead they continue to pass along the trash. In other parts of this book we attempted to present evidence that the unitary system is not failing, it is the policies being mandated by education bureaucrats that are failing the system.

Dual-system reformers often claim that our economy is not competitive enough to conquer the threats posed by China and other emerging markets. The fact is China and its continued manipulation of its currency, the yuan, and iron-fisted control of its poverty-wage labor pool has a greater effect on our economic strength than if every American child scored at the top of every international test, the SAT, the ACT, the GRE, or the MAT. According to Nobel Prize–winning economist Paul Krugman, China's undervaluation of its currency and protectionist policies cost the United States almost 1 million jobs and over 200 billion dollars in lost economic growth and 1.5 percent of its gross domestic product in 2009 (*New York Times*, 2009).

A considerable rise in the value of the yuan would cause U.S. imports to be more economical for Chinese consumers whose yuan is worth more. It becomes a bit of a balancing act because a steep rise (unlikely) will cause China to export inflation to the United States due to an increase in the cost of Chinese goods (Steverman, 2010). Consider as well that just a one-dollar increase in oil drains about 2 percent a year from U.S. GDP. Many factors other than how students score on standardized tests influence economic competitiveness.

Economic strength of the United States and the rest of the G20 countries relies more on policy than education achievement. Tax, trade, health, labor, finance, monetary, housing, and natural resource and energy policies, to name a few, drive our economy, not how students rank on the Trends in International Math and Science Study (TIMSS) or the Programme for International Student Assessment (PISA). To believe otherwise is like believing in the tooth fairy. Reform proposals based on the education/economic connections do not hold up to the existing evidence.

The United States already has one of the highest percentages of people with high school diplomas and college degrees compared to any other country, and we had the largest number of 15-year-old students in the world score at the highest levels on the 2006 PISA science test (OECD, 2008; OECD, 2009; OECD, 2011). We produce more researchers and scientists and qualified engineers than our economy can employ, have even more in the pipeline, and we are one of the most economically competitive nations on the globe (Gereffi & Wadhwa, 2005; Lowell et al., 2009; Council on Competitiveness, 2011; World Economic Forum, 2011).

When trying to extricate the facts from fiction in terms of the relationship between education and economic strength at the global level, it is important to understand that not all economies are created equal (Baker, 2007, 2010; Rameriz, Luo, Schofer & Meyer, 2006; Tienken, 2008). It is not methodologically correct to include every country from the TIMSS or PISA testing samples in the same economic or education pool. The size of the economy matters.

Correlations between test rankings on international tests and economic strength can be statistically significant and moderately strong when all the small or weak economies like Poland, Hungary, and the Slovak Republic remain in the sample with the G20 countries; however, the relationship between international test ranks and economic strength can be nonexistent or even negative when only the G14 or G20 economies, the largest economies in the world, form the sample (Tienken, 2008).

What the myth-spinsters seem not to understand is that nations with strong economies (e.g., the G20) demonstrate a weaker relationship between increases in education attainment on standardized tests and economic growth. Japan provides an example of this phenomenon. Japan's stock market, the Nikkei 225 Average, closed at a high of 38,915 points on December 31, 1989, and on October 15, 2012, it closed at 8,534 points, approximately 80 percent lower. But Japan has ranked in the top 10 on international tests of mathematics since the 1980s and has always ranked higher than the United States on such tests.

Yet Japan's stock market and its economy have been struggling for almost two decades. They have national curriculum standards and testing, and have for over 30 years. Japanese students outrank students in most other nations on math and science tests. In contrast, the Dow Jones Industrial Average broke 1,200 points for the first time on April 26, 1983, the day *A Nation at Risk* (National Commission on Excellence in Education, 1983) was released. The Dow closed at 13,155 points on December 7, 2012, over a tenfold increase. The United States consistently outranks Japan on the World Economic Forum's Growth Competitiveness Index.

So we are still wondering, where is the connection? (See Tienken, 2011.) Maybe Japan's gross domestic product (GDP) benefited from the high rankings on international tests more so than the United States'? Since 1984 the GDP of Japan and the United States have grown at basically the same rates. The United States posted third-quarter GDP in 2010 that was approximately 3.74 times larger than in 1984, whereas Japan's 2010 third-quarter GDP was 3.48 times larger than in 1984. Advantage United States regardless of what some call poor international test rankings.

The United States had approximately two times the number of 15-year-old students who scored at the top levels of the 2006 PISA science test compared to Japan. The United States accounted for 25 percent of the top scoring students in the world on that test, even though the United States did not outrank Japan overall.

For most of the years between 2001–2012, the United States ranked either first or second out of 139 nations on the World Economic Forum's (2010) Global Competitiveness Index (GCI). It never ranked below seventh place during that period, regardless of results on international assessments and without adopting national curriculum standards. No other country has ranked better consistently on the GCI. The U.S. work-force is one of the most productive in the world and best educated.

Approximately 70 percent of recent high school graduates were en-rolled in colleges and universities in 2011 (Bureau of Labor Statistics, 2012). Approximately 33 percent of U.S. adults between ages 25 and 34 years old have at least a bachelor's degree. Only seven other industrial-ized nations have a higher percentage of their population holding at least a bachelor's degree (OECD, 2009), but their economies pale in compari-son to the United States'. The United States leads the world in what are known as utility patents or patents for innovations.

In 2011, the United States was granted 108,626 utility patents, whereas Japan, the country with the next greatest number, was granted 46,139. All the countries of the world combined to achieve 115,879 utility patents, a little over 7,000 more than the U.S. total (U.S. Patent and Trademark Office, 2011).

The United States is home to over 28 percent of the patents granted globally (resident patents), the largest percentage of any country. Japan is second with 20 percent. The United States is second behind Japan for the number of trademarks, 1.7 million versus 1.4 million (World Intellectual Property Organization, 2010). The World Economic Forum (2010) stated that the United States has an outstanding university system. It is home to 11 out of the top 15 universities in the world; the United Kingdom is next with 3 out of 15 (*Times Higher Education*, 2010). It seems illogical that the country with the best university system in the world can have a failing PK-12 education system that needs to be placed under centralized curric-ular control.

The World Economic Forum attributed the fall of the United States from second place to sixth place on the 2010–2011 GCI in large part to increased weakness in auditing and financial reporting standards and a lack of corporate ethics. The overall trust in the U.S. market sophistica-tion has dropped from ninth in the world to 31st between 2010–2012 due to the fact that the global economic meltdown was created by the U.S. financial markets and vended across the globe.

Conspicuously missing from the list of reasons for the U.S. drop in competitiveness was the quality of its education system, because educa-tion does not drive the U.S. economy (World Economic Forum, 2010). Test rankings simply do not correlate to economic strength when one compares apples to apples. Baker (2010) found a -.48 correlation between a country's rank on the First International Mathematics Study (FIMS) in 1964 and its purchasing power parity gross domestic product (PPP-GDP). Rameriz et al. (2006) found very weak positive relationships ranging from .048 to .142, and those positive relationships were mainly for small and weak economies—size still matters.

Tienken (2008) found no statistically significant relationships between the top 22 performing economies in the world and their ranks on international tests of math and science going back to the FIMS. Salzman and Lowell (2008) documented that 90 percent of the variance in test scores on the PISA is explained by factors within countries, not between countries. Why do we focus on a solution that at best will provide only up to a 10 percent improvement?

Where is the evidence that standardizing and centralizing curriculum and assessment policy and practice, merit pay, ending tenure, ending collective bargaining for teachers, high-stakes testing, retaining students in grade, larger class sizes, privatizing the public schools through corporately funded charter schools, expanding the general charter school movement, mayoral control, or allowing the night manager from the local gym who has a bachelor's degree to be a superintendent (see the proposal from New Jersey's governor, Chris Christie, to allow anyone with a bachelor's degree and "management experience" to be a superintendent) are effective? Where is the evidence that national curriculum standards will cause American students to score at the top of international tests or make them more competitive?

Some point to the fact that many of the countries that outrank the United States have national, standardized curricula. Our reply is there are also nations like Canada, Australia, Germany, and Switzerland that have very strong economies, rank higher than the United States on international tests of mathematics and science consistently, and do not have a mandated, standardized set of national curriculum standards. McCluskey (2010) reported that for the 27 nations with complete data sets that outranked the United States on the 2006 PISA science test, 10 of those nations did not have national standards, whereas 12 of the 28 nations that ranked lower than the United States had national standards.

The same pattern of mixed results held true for the 2007 grade 8 TIMSS mathematics results. Although the eight countries that outranked the United States on that test had national standards, so did 33 of the 39 countries that ranked lower (McCluskey, 2010). The students from the majority of nations with national standards ranked lower than the U.S. students. The same pattern held true for the TIMSS science assessment.

More countries with national standards underperformed the United States than did countries without national standards. If people dig a bit, they will find a lack of evidence to support the current wave of dual-system reforms. Why do some so fervently want to believe the myths, lies, and fear in the face of evidence to the contrary? How is that data-driven decision making?

Enough?

There are now enough data and studies available to demonstrate clearly that the current wave of reform is educationally baseless and void of trustworthy conclusions. It is time for those responsible for the well-being of children to play the role. Even the corporately developed Interstate School Leaders Licensure Consortium (ISLLC) standards for school administrators call on school leaders to act in the best interest of children. It might be time to begin prosecuting people for education malpractice who pass legislation, implement reforms that are untested and without significant benefits to children, and force others to do so.

No one can claim ignorance at this point. Those responsible for the well-being of children have a responsibility to know what they are doing. Why is it that schools must demonstrate scientifically based evidence for the interventions they want to use, but policy makers, pundits, and the latest wave of school reformers are allowed to vend ideas based only on ideology and legislate unscientific practices?

WHERE WE CAN GO

We propose some general ideas for a way forward. Because education should be a local endeavor, and many interventions are contextual and need to be customized, we present our ideas not as a recipe, but as part of an overall evidence-based platform from which to launch specific policies and programs at the local level. It is up to those with the courage, ethical fortitude, and the will to save the public schools to develop locally innovative means to connect children to evidence-based practices that will tap into local talents while also propelling students to make global connections. Think of it as local globalism—look globally and act locally.

PROPOSAL PART I: LOCAL CONTROL

Our first preference is to return public education to the public through increased local control. The system of local control produced the positive results described earlier—among others. Most state standards and other state and national controls did not exist prior to 1994, yet the United States produced Nobel Prize winners, more scientists than the economy could employ, unprecedented per-capita income, and the highest standard of living in the world.

Innovation and creativity cannot be mandated from a state-controlled system. Cuba, China, Singapore, and the former Soviet Union serve as just a handful of harsh examples of what happens when local control is stripped from education: creativity is stripped away as well. One reason why China's economy has improved over the last three decades is because it began to allow more localization of the economy. If it takes that approach with its schools, then perhaps we should be worried. China is working hard to get out from under the rock of standardization and into more localization. One of its universities has already started (Zhao, 2011).

In contrast to what the new wave of reformers would have you believe, U.S. schools were able to prepare competent and competitive citizens prior to national and state centralization. This was due in part to the environment of input guarantee policies in which the federal and state governments provided funds to the local districts to deploy based on local needs. The drastic rise during the 1990s of the performance guarantee environment, in which schools had to demonstrate consistent growth in high-stakes test scores (the output variable) as a requirement for receiving funding, has changed the focus and shifted the power to the funding source and away from the local taxpayers.

The performance guarantee creates a system in which schools must work toward centralized goals that do not take into account local needs and strengths. Performance guarantee policies actually stifle creativity because they are often tied to sanctions that create fear. Teachers and administrators are afraid to try new programs for fear that their test scores will decline. The performance guarantee environment increases the chances of massive swings of the pendulum based on ideology and politics, instead of local movements that are more open to deliberation.

Performance guarantee environments lead to the invisible hand from afar directing the workings of the local. They allow a small group of elites to guide an entire system. Not all towns are created equal, and the conditions on the ground can change dramatically; even within the span of a few square miles. Yong Zhao (2010) described the approach to return public education to the public as "mass localism." He explains that local control is the key to creativity because each locale can address its needs through customized solutions that draw on evidence-based practices and ideas.

Each locale can express its local interests while exposing its children to the larger world through technology-enabled collaboration. Zhao's ideas have a strong empirical base of support from deep in education's history. The ideas flow from the experimentalist philosophy and an acknowledgment of the learner as an active constructor of meaning who has prior knowledge and needs to connect that prior knowledge to new learning in developmentally appropriate and authentic situations.

Of course we have the mountains of curricular knowledge created by Francis Parker, John Dewey, Horace Mann, Ralph Tyler, Boyd Bode, the Harap Committee, and Hilda Taba to support ideas like Zhao's and to pierce the veil of secrecy that surrounds many of the standardization policies and reform practices. We have large empirical studies from others as well.

The landmark Eight-Year Study demonstrated that curriculum can be an entirely locally developed project and still produced better results in high school and then in college than traditional curricular programs (Aikin, 1942). In fact, the experiment demonstrated that the less standardized, more diverse, locally developed and designed the programs (based on demonstrated research and theories of learning), the better the students did in college academically, socially, and civically compared their traditionally prepared peers.

Results from several other well-known earlier studies demonstrated that there is not "one best curriculum path" for students in high school, and standardized curricula sequences are not necessary to achieve superior results in elementary and high schools (Collings & Kilpatrick, 1929; Jersild, Thorndike & Goldman, 1941; Thorndike, 1924; Wrightstone, Rechetnick, McCall & Loftus, 1939).

Developmentally Appropriate and Relevant Curriculum

Locally developed standards could certainly play a role in future reforms. We are not advocating that a set of locally developed rigid standards replace the current set of national and state-imposed standards. We are floating the idea that standards, when developed at a cognitively, socially, and morally appropriate level and used as guidance, could help to structure a comprehensive, creative local curriculum. We return to the cognitive development chart presented in earlier chapters to support our idea.

Consider the following kindergarten mastery mathematics standard from the Common Core State Standards Initiative in light of the cognitive development chart (see table 9.1):

- Compose and decompose numbers from 11 to 19 into ten ones and some further ones, e.g., by using objects or drawings, and record each composition or decomposition by a drawing or equation (such as $18 = 10 + 8$); understand that these numbers are composed of ten ones and one, two, three, four, five, six, seven, eight, or nine ones.

Although there is room for debate, this standard seems to reside somewhere between Early Concrete and Advanced Concrete development, depending on how it will be assessed: multiple choice, close-end short response, or open-ended and whether students can use concrete objects or must use abstract symbols.

What is not a question is whether this is expected to be mastered by 100 percent of kindergarten students as part of the CCSS initiative. It is expected to be mastered because the CCSS are mastery standards. To receive full credit the student would probably have to move from pic-

Table 9.1. **Cognitive Development Chart**

Age	Grade	Intuition	Early Concrete (a)	Advanced Concrete (b)	Entry Formal (a)	Middle Formal (b)	Ref.
5.5	P	78	22				J
6	K	68	27	5			A
7	1	35	55	10			A, W
8	2	25	55	20			A
9	3	15	55	30			A
10	4	12	52	35	1		S
11	5	6	49	40	5		S
12	6–7	5	32	51	12		S
13	7–8	2	34	44	14	6	S
14	8–9	1	32	43	15	9	S
15	9–10	1	15	53	18	13	S
16	10–11	1	13	50	17	19	S
16–17	11–12	3	19	47	19	12	R
17–18	12	1	15	50	15	19	R
Adult	—	20	22	26	17	15	R

Source: Herman T. Epstein, personal communication, June 8, 1999. See also Epstein 2002.

Level (a) in each category is composed of children who have just begun to manifest one or two of that level's reasoning schemes, while level (b) refers to children manifesting a half dozen or more reasoning schemes.

A—Arlin, P. Personal communication with H. T. Epstein.

J—Smedslund, J. (1964). *Concrete Reasoning: A Study of Intellectual Development.* Lafayette, IN: Child Development Publications of the Society for Research in Child Development.

R—Renner, J. W., Stafford, D. G., Lawson, A. E., McKinnon, J. W., Friot, F. E. & Kellogg, D. H. (1976). *Research, Teaching and Learning with the Piaget Model.* Norman: University of Oklahoma Press.

S—Shayer, M. & Adey, P. (1981). *Towards a Science of Science Teaching.* London: Heinemann.

W—Wei, T. D. et al. (1971). Piaget's Concept of Classification: A Comparative Study of Socially Disadvantaged and Middle-Class Young Children. *Child Development* (42): 919–927.

tures to symbolic representation, and thus, show through a set of symbols how to construct the various numbers, as shown in the example. Therefore, to receive full credit, the student would be operating more in Advanced Concrete than Early Concrete.

The problem arises because many kindergarten children are not operating at the Early or Advanced Concrete levels developmentally. That does not mean schools should not expose students to that level of work. In fact they should. However, it is developmentally dangerous and professionally reckless to require all students to master standards that lie outside of normal human cognitive development when less than half of the national kindergarten population operates consistently and at a mastery level in the advanced Concrete stage of development.

Students should be exposed to challenging content. Vygotsky (1978) demonstrated that students can access and work with challenging content with the guidance of a teacher, through guided practice, but that content needs to be within the "zone of proximal development" of the student. Even with the help of a teacher, it is still foolish to believe that all students can MASTER all these concepts if they are not developmentally ready. Yes, they can learn many of them, and should be exposed to them, but they should not be made to master that which they are not developmentally equipped to handle.

Local entities should be held responsible for developing challenging curriculum and assessments that capitalize on local strengths, address local needs, and prepare students for a globalized world, but those standards must be based on what is known about cognitive development. The curriculum should reflect the broad goals that the general public, school board members, and state legislators identified as being important.

Those broad goals include (a) basic academic skills and knowledge, (b) critical thinking, (c) appreciation for arts and literature, (d) preparation for skilled employment, (e) social skills and a general work ethic, (f) citizenship, and (g) physical and emotional health (Rothstein, Jacobsen & Wilder, 2008, p. 43). Could educators still use standards as a guide and adopt standards at the local level? Of course they can.

We recommend that an evaluation of the cognitive complexity of each standard be conducted to ensure that the standards are developmentally appropriate. Then the standards can act as a skeleton upon which to build a more complete curriculum. Some districts might choose some of the CCSS along with some of their state standards, locally developed goals and objectives, recommendations from national curriculum associations, and perhaps some standards from another country. It depends on the district's goals, the students' needs, and the community's vision for education. It does not have to be an "either/or" decision, but the decision does need to be cognitively appropriate, and requirements for mastery (formal state assessments) must match the cognitive developmental level of the students.

Once again, we are not saying that the curriculum should not extend, challenge, and enrich students. It should, and it should span multiple cognitive developmental stages so as to ensure equity (all children getting what they need, not getting the same). But assessing mastery via standardized assessments in which results are used to make high-stakes decisions should be determined by testing only those standards that reside in the cognitive level in which all children without cognitive disabilities reside or have exited.

Using table 9.1 as an example, about 85 percent of the students without cognitive disabilities in grade 3 would be expected to master standards at the early concrete level, and the test items should reflect that cognitive level. Schools can and should augment those mastery standards with other standards that support and extend learning and assess them at the local level. Then they can use the results from the mastery assessment plus their local assessments to develop a clearer picture of student learning.

A logical question one should ask is how does this type of curriculum account for the various cognitive levels that can exist at any age or grade level? We believe the curriculum activities for each standard and/or objective can be differentiated—tiered, to include two or three levels of cognitive complexity. The activities used to teach students and to assess their understanding can include two or three cognitive tiers. Teachers who differentiate their instruction by "readiness" already know about this. It is an idea that has been around for about 100 years, first proposed formally in the Cardinal Principles of Secondary Education (Commission on Reorganization of Secondary Education, 1918).

There is no need to guess anymore what constitutes a worthwhile curriculum. Replace "rigor" with "relevance" and "arbitrary" with "cognitively appropriate." In order for transfer of knowledge to occur there must be immediate relevance. Learning material because it might appear on a test is not relevant, no matter how high the stakes. Thorndike's studies (1901; 1924) demonstrated clearly that achievement in one subject area does not automatically transfer to another area. Transfer has to be facilitated by meaningful and purposeful connection of content areas to each other and to the student.

Content not connected to the experiences and needs of the students subjected to that content is irrelevant and counterproductive at worst. Not only do more children learn less, disconnected, isolated content breeds discontent among the most dispossessed and fragile of our children: the poor living on the margins of society in our urban centers.

Those dispossessed by the larger society are only going to take so much in terms of having irrelevant content heaped upon them before they drop out or react in other ways. The Report of the National Advisory Commission on Civil Disorders (1968), also known as the Kerner Commission, created as a result of the many riots in U.S. cities during the late 1960s, found that a lack of meaningful, relevant, responsive curriculum was an issue contributing to poverty and unrest in the cities. Content without a conscious connection to the student is just another recipe for failure.

LOCALLY GROWN

The problem-based, socially conscious curriculum was demonstrated to be superior to traditional forms and needs to be returned to the classroom, through local development. It should come as no surprise that our best medical and nursing schools use problem-based curricula. If it is good enough for some of our most important professionals that care for children, why is it not good enough for our children? Curriculum organization must blend the subject matter disciplines with student experiences and concerns.

There must be a fusion of subject matter with the student, and the student must be viewed as an active constructor of meaning who brings prior knowledge and experience to the learning environment; that prior knowledge and experience must be used as a springboard and connection to the new material (Dewey, 1938; Taba, 1962; Tanner & Tanner, 2007; Tyler, 1950).

Curriculum deliberation, development, and implementation are proximal variables (Wang, Haertel & Walberg, 1993). Curriculum design has the greatest influence on learning when it is created closer to the student—at the local level. Curriculum must be designed and developed collaboratively and locally, by the teachers, administrators, and students who use and experience it, to have the greatest influence (Tanner & Tanner, 2007; Tramaglini, 2010; Wang, Haertel & Walberg, 1993). The design and organization of the curriculum at the local level were two of the strongest administratively mutable variables identified by Wang, Haertel, and Walberg (1993) that affected student achievement.

Curriculum development that influences student achievement has a demonstrated history of residing at the local level and a demonstrated track record of influencing student academic, emotional, and social successes. State governance and policy setting is one of the weakest variables in terms of student development (Wang et al., 1993). We wonder about the influence of national governance in what used to be a locally controlled system, and we question the motives of those who support a distal approach to curriculum development and implementation.

Standards are not evil. Cognitively inappropriate standards that all students must master are problematic. We believe general standards based on developmental psychological evidence can be informative for local decision makers and provide one piece of guidance. They can act as a starting point or a framework from which innovative practices can emanate. They should not be the ends, just another part of the means.

Unity of purpose, a quality education for all, need not result in uniformity in curriculum, instruction, and assessment. We must jettison the notion that all students must master the same information. Knowledge creation is not a passive endeavor built upon static and inert curriculum standards. This requires that educators have a deep understanding of their students on the macro level, the community and school environment, and culture of various groups. They must also have microunderstanding of their students; they must know their students at the student level in order to customize programs and curriculum (Vygotsky, 1978). The power of relationships cannot be overstated.

PROPOSAL PART II: ASSESSMENT

Information from cognitive psychology and the existing knowledge of the stages of cognitive development have implications for any testing connected to standards. The local development of curriculum standards requires locally developed assessments in order to customize the learning experiences for all children. Once again, education has a strong history of developing comprehensive assessment systems that do not rely on state-mandated standardized tests. As we presented in chapter 6, numerous negative issues surround the continued use of state-mandated tests of academic skills and knowledge.

Assessment does not have to be based on a narrow definition of student achievement focused only on atomized academic content. It can be, and historically has been, much more than that. In some ways the current mainstream policy conception of assessment is intellectually, emotionally, socially, and culturally regressive. It does not move humanity forward. It is essentialist in its philosophical framework and seeks to place knowledge and skills into predetermined discipline-centered compartments, independent of context and void of use in authentic problems. The current state of education assessment affairs does not have to continue on this course. We need only look to our rich past of education research to see a way forward.

We stand on the precipice of returning to the broken system Horace Mann and Francis Parker exposed over 150 years ago. A culturally and intellectually deprived system of training, not education, that lacks a social consciousness. A system based on measurement and not based on inquiry or growth. But it does not have to be this way.

We can have a heightened focus on results and an expanded definition of achievement with local flavor and global sophistication. If we only knew our history as a profession or chose to learn from it, we would know of an example from a consortium of high schools across the country that jettisoned the bankrupt practice of standardized testing and instead created locally responsive and broad measures of social, emotional, and academic student growth.

An Assessment Collage

After the 30 high schools and districts that were involved in the Eight-Year Study (Aikin, 1942) made the decision to cut the standardized testing cord, they were left to develop a more comprehensive system. They could not rely on the prophesized ease of making decisions from just one test per year. They actually had to take stock of their educational goals and objectives and develop a system to meet them; 30 unique systems for 30 unique populations with one common goal of creating quality education programs to develop well-rounded citizens.

Quality programs require quality feedback. Below is a partial list of the summative assessments developed and used during the Eight-Year Study, their reliability estimates, and whether they were useful for individual student diagnosis or diagnosis of groups (see table 9.2).

Over 150 assessments, summative and formative, were eventually used with students during the study (see table 9.2).

The majority of the assessments used during the Eight-Year Study were not developed by assessment corporations or organizations. They

Table 9.2.   High-Reliability Assessments Developed for the Eight-Year Study

Assessment Title	Grades Assessed	Reliability Estimate	Use with Individual (I) or Group (G)
Ability to Make Original Interpretations (of Data)	7–8	.85	I or G
Application of Principles of Logical Reasoning	9–12	.94	I or G
Tests on Beliefs of Social Issues	11–12	.85	I or G
Analysis of Controversial Writing (Propaganda)	10–12	.70–.82	I or G
Art Appreciation	12	.77	I or G
Personal and Social Adjustment	7–12	.75–.78	I or G

Data source: Aikin, W. M. (1942). *The Story of the Eight-Year Study.* New York: Harper.

were developed by a collaboration of teachers, school administrators, and university faculty in what are now known as professional learning communities. Although it is true that some "off-the-shelf" psychological tests were used to assess some aspects of social and emotional development, the vast majority of the assessments used were created by educators for students. This partial list of assessments provides evidence that we need not rely on the current system of myopic tests vended to us at much cost. It is possible for educators to develop high-quality assessments that produce fine-grained, diagnostic results.

The reliability estimates are stronger than many of those found on the subsections of most state-mandated tests. Because the staff members were concerned with developing an education experience that attended to the social, emotional, and academic needs of all students, they recognized the need to develop feedback loops to inform instructional and leadership decision making.

Standardized tests that are developmentally appropriate can play a part in a comprehensive assessment system, but simply as another data point among many. Their results should not be given any greater consideration than the results from other locally developed assessments. Other assessments included:

- Social Sensitivity
- Ability to Apply Social Facts and Generalizations
- Democratic Values
- Applying Facts and Generalizations to Social Problems
- Evaluation of Social Attitudes
- Beliefs on Economic Issues
- Student Reading Inventory
- Student Reaction to Reading
- Questionnaire on Voluntary Reading
- Critical Mindedness in the Reading of Fiction
- Judging the Effectiveness of Written Composition
- The Novel Questionnaire
- The Drama Questionnaire
- Evaluation of Literature
- Student Interest Inventory
- Socially Conscious Problem Solving

But these ideas are not lost in education's past. They were used successfully in recent times. The Nebraska STARS (School-based Teacher-led Assessment and Reporting System) has been in place in Nebraska since 2000 and until approximately 2004–2005 it relied on local assessments graded by teachers (Dappen & Isernhagen, 2005; Roschewski, Isernhagen & Dappen, 2006).

When the STARS system was first developed, the Nebraska department of education required that districts either adopt the state-approved core standards or create their own set of standards that were at least of the same quality. Districts that opted for the local option could also develop a local set of assessments to demonstrate evidence of student learning (Dappen & Isernhagen, 2005).

The state's department of education acted as a support system with professional development in how to design various assessments, how to design and use rubrics, how to report assessment results, and how to interpret the results to inform instruction. The department of education also acted as part of the auditing process in terms of helping to ensure assessment quality. This locally developed curriculum and assessment system was in place for approximately seven years until a new superintendent of state instruction chose to follow a traditional approach to implementing NCLB. The STARS system stands as the modern-day example that localism can work on a large scale (there are over 500 school districts in Nebraska).

Support Local Development

If American presidents and policy makers really want us to innovate and be competitive, then they should support the expansion of local control, not the submission of local control to a nationally directed system that is slow and lumbering. It is all about turning radius. Our systems need to be able to change directions quickly and be nimble. We liken it to boating. It takes a considerable amount of time for a long-haul container ship to execute a 270-degree turn, whereas a 35-foot recreational boat can do it in seconds.

Some groups in the United States have been trying to impose tanker-like national standards on public schools for over 30 years. Look what we got—nineteenth-century standards copied almost directly from the Committees of Ten and Fifteen, circa 1893 and 1895. At this pace it will take another two hundred years to get standards turned around that begin to address current needs. Instead, we should unleash the power of innovation locally.

Hold policy makers, school leaders, and teachers accountable for authentic, innovative student learning. There exists today no accountability for student learning in the current summative high-stakes system. High-stakes standardized tests are easy to game due to the multiple test preparation packages available for every state test. It is easy to go through state standards and identify which standards are actually testable using current low-quality instruments and which are not. It is easy to determine the format and level of difficulty of the possible items. Then, one just has to narrow the curriculum to the most likely tested items in the most likely tested formats. That is not education, and that is not innovative student learning.

Hold schools accountable for developing a basket of assessments, quantitative and qualitative, that demonstrate student academic, social, emotional, and innovative achievements, and that allow for diversity in achievement while operating within a developmentally appropriate curriculum. Create a continuum of growth rubrics for measuring progress holistically over time.

The goal is not to have students arrive at a finite point, but instead to demonstrate growth over time. School leaders and teachers will have to grapple with this idea since they have very little experience synthesizing solutions to open-ended problems like assessing student growth and innovation. However, they need only take a page out of the Eight-Year Study (Aikin, 1942) for guidance. Policy makers must provide the intellectual space to allow this system to develop, and that space will only be brought about by an uprising by the, until now, unsuspecting public and a return to an input guarantee environment to spur innovation.

PROPOSAL PART III: ADDRESS THE ROOT CAUSES OF UNDERACHIEVEMENT

The public education system, the country's largest social infrastructure, does not drive society, it reflects it. Therefore, any reform of education must include social reforms. The latest wave of reformers claim they are concerned with underachievement, especially for students of color and those that come from poverty. That is an interesting concern in light of the fact that poverty is the largest predictor of ultimate academic achievement on traditional standardized tests in this country. We wonder why recent reforms ignore the major driver of academic achievement.

Although there is a weak to a negative correlation, depending on the study, between how a country ranked on the latest PISA math test and overall country gross domestic product, there is a statistically significant ($p < .05$) Spearman Rho correlation (.274) between a country's income inequality and its rank on PISA math: The more unequal the distribution of income in a country, the lower a country ranked on the PISA, in general.

Condron (2011) found a strong, statistically significant ($p = .05$) relationship between income inequity and scores on the PISA 2006 mathematics and science tests. According to the CIA World Factbook (2011) the United States has an income distribution score of 45 and a rank of 94th out of 135 ranked countries. Sweden was ranked 1st for equitable income distribution with a score of 23. Countries that ranked near the United States included Iran, Nigeria, Cameroon, Uganda, and Uruguay (Iran and Nigeria actually had more equal distributions of income than the United States).

We are not going to argue about reasons for income inequality. We are simply stating that all students cannot achieve to their fullest potential if some groups are disadvantaged by the negative factors associated with poverty. True education reform cannot occur without social reform. The health-related issues associated with poverty are more than enough to impede appropriate cognitive growth.

Children of poverty are more than twice as likely to be plagued with chronic illnesses, preventable disabilities, low cognitive functioning and learning disabilities, dental problems, hearing and sight issues, and heart and digestive system disorders (Currie, 2005). They are almost two times as likely to need emotional and behavioral services compared to their nonpoor peers (U.S. Department of Health and Human Services, 2004). They underachieve their nonpoor peers, as a group, on every state-mandated academic test of skills and knowledge (Tienken, 2011).

Children of poverty lack fundamental supports that the more wealthy access on a regular basis. For example, appropriate, center-based child care (Loch et al., 2004) has a positive influence on cognitive development and academic achievement, as does universal health care. Children of poverty have less frequent access to both. In contrast, the G20 nations that outscored the United States on the 2009 PISA math had universal health care for children or universal child care, or a combination of both (except China, as only the city of Shanghai participated and thus is not counted as a country).

Schwartz (2010) demonstrated that appropriate housing policy affects student achievement more than the education interventions being proposed by the latest crop of reformistas. Many children of poverty live in substandard housing in neighborhoods that are less than conducive to cognitive, social, and emotional growth. Some opponents of liberty and justice for all might retort that America can't afford to do the things necessary to alleviate the negative effects of poverty. Not true.

Gale and Kotlikoff (2004, pp. 1288–1290) estimated that if the Bush II–era tax cuts were not allowed to continue, there would have been net gain to government revenue, the amount equal to 2 percent of GDP, and that alone would have been more than enough to provide meaningful support to poor children. But that did not happen, and instead, the wealthiest 2 percent of all Americans received another income benefit, a cash payment if you will.

Gale and Kotlikoff concluded there would have been enough money for indigent families to provide: (a) an increase in the child allowance cash payment to bring families to or above the poverty line, (b) comprehensive prenatal and perinatal screenings, (c) universal health coverage for children up to the age of 18, (d) universal preschool, (e) center-based child care so families can work, (f) equitable parent leave programs to care for newborns and sick children, and (g) services for emotionally and behaviorally disturbed children, among other productive measures. Add in even a portion of the 130 billion dollars a year the United States has been spending since 2003 on wars in Iraq and Afghanistan, and there certainly seems to be enough money. What we lack is the moral conscience and courage to do something.

It seems undemocratic to deny a group of people full access to the democratic society due to the preexisting condition of poverty or an unanticipated fall into poverty. Of course there are those who blame poverty on the poor and a lack of work ethic. Unfortunately, that argument breaks down quickly when one realizes there are not enough available jobs that pay a living wage to employ everyone. Therefore, it is in the interest of the greater good to support those who find themselves without a living wage, with a living wage. They are consumers as well, and the money distributed to the poor will find its way back into the system through the capitalist economic process and thus generate tax revenue and added wealth.

PROPOSAL PART IV: REFOCUS THE ROLE OF THE U.S. DEPARTMENT OF EDUCATION

The appropriate role of the federal government in public education needs redefining. It is the purpose of this section to redefine that role in light of historical precedents. The U.S. Constitution is silent on the topic of education. However, the Tenth Amendment has been interpreted by the courts as giving the respective states jurisdiction over public education.

Over the past five decades, the federal government has moved into educational control through a mechanism called "categorical aid." The ESEA Act is now the guiding policy for use of punishment to encroach on the Tenth Amendment interpretation. It is time to reassess the current model of categorical aid and reengineer the federal role to a more streamlined one.

To initiate the reengineering effort, the role of the federal government should be clarified and simplified. Federal policy should be instituted to provide block categorical grants to all states and territories where federal legislation has had direct impact on instruction. There are three areas where the federal government should provide majority financial support: (a) vocational education, (b) special education, and (c) preschool education.

The above-listed areas have massive costs and programs associated with them because federal laws and subsequent regulations require states to incur greater expenses than they would if there were no federal policy. Thus, the three are identified for primary and categorical support.

Funding

The second action would be to make one general aid grant to each state and territory based on population as an input guarantee. This would allow a return to the input guarantee approach that could jump-start innovation at the local level—mass localism as advocated by Zhao and demonstrated effective by the giants of the experimentalist movement. The input guarantee grants would help to equalize the wealth of richer and poorer states, similar to forward-looking state financial equalization programs. A special grant would go to urban schools to alleviate those unique problems. A similar special grant might also go to rural and isolated schools.

Input guarantees can be differentiated based on the contexts of the school districts and schools that receive them. They can be customized because the local districts and schools have control. Of course there might be some parameters such as the majority of the funds need to be used for innovative practices in curriculum, instruction, and informing student learning, but the parameters would be general in nature as to not stifle creativity. These funds cannot be manipulated by state legislators to fund pet projects or ideological follies. They should flow directly to the districts themselves with the state as the conduit, not as an extortionist.

A newly constituted Federal Office of Education could be housed in the Department of Health and Human Services (DHHS). DHHS is a natural location for FOE because DHHS is involved in childhood policy issues and input from DHHS officials might prove helpful. The FOE could have a division for international liaison, to help spur global innovations in local districts. The International Division would also act as a conduit for our world neighbors as a point of access for collaboration.

The usual statistical gathering and assessing programs, such as NAEP and the National Center for Education Statistics (NCES), would also be kept at the national level and all moved appropriately. The NCES could be assigned to the U.S. Bureau of the Census. Other federal departments or agencies, such as the Department of Agriculture, the Department of Justice, the Bureau of Indian Affairs, the National Science Foundation, and several others in the executive branch, would need to coordinate and redefine their roles in educational policymaking and program operations.

The Plus Side

Our plan has at least six positive attributes. The federal role in education becomes manageable and accountable. Legislatures and local school boards will determine public education policy with school boards retaining the right to view legislation as guidance only in terms of what is taught, how it is taught, and how it is assessed.

Federal and state legislators would concern themselves with ensuring only safety and civil rights and enforcement of equality and equity laws for students, not legislating compensation systems, mandating instructional practices or products, or creating dual systems vis-à-vis taking tax money and giving it to charter schools. They can require that districts have some type of system to demonstrate students are learning, but they should not mandate a one-size-fits-all output. Raise the level of accountability by having districts "prove" that they are innovating through triannual innovation showcases. Perhaps allowing districts to move away from an assessment system toward an "Innovation Configuration" to demonstrate student achievements in many areas would spur further innovation.

The massive federal education bureaucracy would be reduced. Local and state education authorities would be freed from micromanagement and countless worker hours to complete lengthy, but trivial, questionnaires, complex forms, and meaningless certifications.

Educationally nonproductive federal categorical "giveaways" would be eliminated and allow for large inflows of redeployed cash for input guarantee innovation funding. The areas we propose for direct support—vocational, special, and early childhood education—are now controlled by federal laws and regulations. The Congress has directed states and even schoolteachers how to conduct classes. The federal government should, therefore, pay the full cost of program implementation. Success of these national mandates would be in the nation's best interest as well.

The NCLB Act has catapulted categorical aid out of control and rendered it ineffective by tightly controlling how it is used. It must be dramatically reduced or eliminated to free the states of meddlesome federal bureaucrats. The new role of the federal government would be to encourage excellence in public education, not to tinker with it for continued conflict. We call for a commitment to a comprehensive approach to public educational policy.

Our plan requires a new pledge to the American people for public schools that teach and students who learn, and it provides a renewed social contract with America's youth. If the twenty-first century is to usher in new hope to all who deserve the best public educational systems in the world, then this is the very least we can do—perhaps the most.

POINTS TO REMEMBER

The words of the democratic reformers like Mann (1848), along with Dewey, Parker, Tyler, and the other giants of our field sometimes fall on deaf ears, but there is no more urgent task that faces school leaders than to safeguard liberty and justice for all. Some of our colleagues say it is useless to fight the current wave of data-less reforms like standardization and testing and that they will continue to be useless until policy makers adopt a more enlightened attitude toward evidence and science.

But we believe we can help educators and those who care about children to begin the change process by looking inward at the ideas and ideologies educators support and implement. Those who care about the democratic future of children need to examine their ideas and be willing to acknowledge that perhaps they hold beliefs born from worn-out slogans and dogmas. We, the authors of this book, need to heed our own admonitions. We too need to jettison ideas that rest only on rhetoric and hold no hope for children. Let us focus our efforts on demonstrated interventions.

Let us not be silent. We draw on the thoughts of Martin Luther King to support our voices of dissent about current policies when he said, "In the end, we will remember not the words of our enemies, but the silence of our friends." And we remember the words of Robert Kennedy to push us to consider policies that might seem "extreme" or Pollyanna in their proposals for a way forward: "Some see things and ask why, I see things that could be and ask why not."

REFERENCES

Aikin, W. M. (1942). *The Story of the Eight-Year Study*. New York: Harper.

Baker, K. (2007). Are International Tests Worth Anything? *Phi Delta Kappan* 89(2): 101–104.

Baker, K. (2010). A Bad Idea: National Standards Based on Test Scores. *AASA Journal of Scholarship and Practice* 7(3): 60–67.

Bureau of Labor Statistics. (2012, April 19). College enrollment and work activity of 2011 high school graduates. Author. Retrieved from www.bls.gov/news.release/hsgec.nr0.htm.

Callahan, R. E. (1962). *The Cult of Efficiency*. Chicago: The University of Chicago Press.

CIA World Factbook. (2011). Distribution of family income: The GINI index. Author. Retrieved from cs.fit.edu/~ryan/factbook/factbook/rankorder/2172rank.html?countryName=Malaysia&countryCode=my&regionCode=eas&rank=36#my.

Collings, E. & Kilpatrick, W. H. (1929). An Experiment with a Project Curriculum. New York: Macmillan.

Commission on the Reorganization of Secondary Education. (1918). *Cardinal Principles of Secondary Education*. Washington, DC: U.S. Bureau of Education, Bulletin No. 35.

Condron, D. J. (2011). Egalitarianism and Educational Excellence: Compatible Goals for Affluent Societies? *Educational Researcher* 40(2): 47–55.

Council on Competitiveness. (2011). Making impact. Author. Retrieved from www.compete.org/images/uploads/File/PDFpercent20Files/FINAL_IMPACT_2010-2011.pdf.

Currie, J. (2005). Health Disparities and Gaps in School Readiness. *Future of Children* 15(1): 117–138.

Dappen, L. & Isernhagen, J. C. (2005). Nebraska STARS: Assessment for Learning. *Planning and Changing*, 36(3&4): 147–156.

Dewey, J. (1938). *Experience and Education*. New York: Macmillan.

Fuller, B., Wright, J., Gesicki, K. & Kang, E. (2007). Gauging Growth: How to Judge No Child Left Behind? *Educational Researcher* 36(5): 268–278.

Gale, W. & Kotlikoff, L. (2004, June 7). Effects of Recent Fiscal Policies on Children. *Tax Notes*.

Gereffi, G. & Wadhwa, V. (2005). Framing the engineering outsourcing debate: Placing the United States on a level playing field with China and India. Master of Engineering Management Program, Duke University.

Jersild, A. T., Thorndike, R. L. & Goldman, B. (1941). A Further Comparison of Pupils in "Activity" and "Non-Activity" Schools. *Journal of Experimental Education* 9: 307–309.

Loch, S., Fuller, B., Kagan, S. & Carrol, B. (2004). Child Care in Poor Communities: Early Learning Effects of Type, Quality, and Stability. *Child Development* 75(1), 47–65.

Lowell, B. L., Salzman, H., Bernstein, H. & Henderson, E. (2009). *Steady as she goes: Three generations of students through the science and engineering pipeline*. Paper presented at the annual meeting of the Association for Public Policy Management, November 7, 2009, Washington, DC. Retrieved from policy.rutgers.edu/faculty/salzman/SteadyAsSheGoes.pdf.

Mann, H. (1848). *Twelfth annual report of the board of education together with the twelfth annual report of the secretary of the board*. Boston, MA: Dutton and Wentworth State Printers.

McCluskey, N. (2010, February 17). *Behind the curtain. Assessing the case for national standards*. Policy Analysis, 661. Cato Institute. Retrieved from www.cato.org/pubs/pas/pa661.pdf.

National Commission on Excellence in Education. (1983). *A Nation at Risk*. Washington, DC: U.S. Department of Education.

New York Times (December 31, 2009). Krugman also estimates that China's currency policy has caused 1.4 million job losses in the United States.krugman.blogs.nytimes.com/2009/12/31/macroeconomic-effects-of-chinese-mercantilism/.

Organization for Co-Operation and Economic Development [OECD] (2008). *Education at a glance, 2007*. Author.

Organization for Co-Operation and Economic Development [OECD] (2009). *Top of the class: High performers in science in PISA 2006*. Author.

Organization for Co-Operation and Economic Development [OECD] (2011). *Education at a glance, 2010*. Author.

Rameriz, F. O., Luo, X., Schofer, E. & Meyer, J. W. (2006). Student Achievement and National Economic Growth. *American Journal of Education* 113: 1–29.

Roschewski, P., Isernhagen, J. C. & Dappen, L. (2006). Nebraska STARS: Achieving results. *Phi Delta Kappan* 87(6): 433–437.

Rothstein, R., Jacobsen, R. & Wilder, T. (2008). *Grading education: Getting accountability right*. Washington, DC, and New York: Economic Policy Institute and Teachers College Press.

Salzman, H. & Lowell, L. (2008). Making the Grade. *Nature* 453: 28–30.

Schwartz, H. (2010). Housing policy is school policy: Economic integrative housing promotes academic success in Montgomery County, Maryland. New York: The Century Foundation.

Steverman, B. (2010). How a Rising Yuan Could Affect U.S. Investors. *Business Week*.

Taba, H. (1962). *Curriculum Development: Theory into Practice*. New York: Harcourt, Brace, & World, Inc.

Tanner, D. (1971). *Secondary Curriculum*. New York: Macmillan.

Tanner, D. & L. Tanner. (2007). *Curriculum Development: Theory into Practice*. New York: Allyn & Bacon.

Thorndike, E. L. (1924). Mental Discipline in High School Studies. *Journal of Educational Psychology* 15: 1–22, 98.

Thorndike, E. L. & Woodworth, R. S. (1901). The influence of improvement in one mental function upon efficiency of other functions. *Psychological Review* 8: 247–261, 384–395, 553–564.

Tienken, C. H. (2011). Structured Inequity: The Intersection of Socioeconomic Status and the Standard Error of Measurement of State Mandated High School Test Results. NCPEA Yearbook, 257–271.

Tienken, C. H. (2008). Rankings of International Achievement Test Performance and Economic Strength: Correlation or Conjecture. *International Journal of Education Policy and Leadership* 3(4): 1–15.

Tramaglini, T. (2010). *Student achievement in lower SES high schools.* Unpublished doctoral dissertation, Rutgers University.

Tyler, R. W. (1950). *Basic Principles of Curriculum and Instruction.* Chicago: The University of Chicago Press.

United States. (1968). Kerner Commission, Report of the National Advisory Commission on Civil Disorders. Washington: U.S. Government Printing Office.

United States Patent and Trademark Office. (2011). *Calendar year patent statistics: January 1–December 31. By type of patent document.* Author. Retrieved from www.uspto.gov/web/offices/ac/ido/oeip/taf/reports.htm#by_type.

U.S. Department of Health and Human Services: Health Resources and Services Administration. (2004). *The National Survey of Children with Special Health Care Needs Chartbook,* 2001. Rockville, MD: Author.

Vygotsky, L. (1978). *Mind in Society: The Development of Higher Psychological Processes.* Cambridge, MA: Harvard University Press.

Wang, M. C., Haertel, G. D. & Walberg, H. J. (1993). Toward a Knowledge Base for School Learning. *Review of Educational Research* 63(3): 249–294.

World Economic Forum. (2011). *The global competitiveness report 2010–2011.* Houndmills, England: Palgrave Macmillan.

Wrightstone, J. W., Rechetnick, J., McCall, W. A. & Loftus, J. J. (1939). Measuring Social Performance Factors in Activity and Control Schools of New York City. *Teachers College Record* 40(5): 423–432.

Zhao, Y. (2010, May 23). Mass localism: How might the Race To The Top money be better spent. Retrieved from zhaolearning.com/2010/05/23/mass-localism-how-might-the-race-to-the-top-money-be-better-spent/.

Zhao, Y. (2011, March 6). A bold education experiment: What we should learn from China. Retrieved from zhaolearning.com/2011/03/06/a-bold-education-experiment-what-we-should-learn-from-china/.

Index